Christianity and Ethnicity

Is Christ Concerned About Race?

Joyce Reba Payne

Published by:
Lulu.com

Author:
Joyce Reba Payne
P.O. Box 3325
Durham, NC 27702
United States of America

ISBN: 978-1-387-18825-3

Copies available from local bookstores and author website at http://www.lulu.com/spotlight/jrpaynebooks2go.

Contents

Foreword 5
Racial Variations and Complexities 7
Ethnicity in Our Communities 8
Diversities Came Because of Unified Evil 10
Establishment of Christian Religion 10
Christian Gospel First Directed to Ethnic Community 12
- **Evangelism 12**
- **How Did Jesus Teach Witnessing? 13**
- **Why We Misunderstood What Jesus Taught? 14**
- **Old and New Testament Scripture Reveals Recipient of the Message 15**

Why Jesus Originally Limited His Message to His Own People? 17
- **Abrahamic Covenant Fulfilled 18**
- **Requirement of Faithfulness 22**
- **Requirement of Identification 27**
- **Qualification for Priesthood 30**

Why Is It Important to Minister to One's Own Culture First? 35
- **Prophet to the People 36**
- **Ensample for the People 40**

How Non-Ethnic Ministers Can Present Difficulty for Ethnic Congregation? 44
Every Nation Must Be Reconciled Back to God 51
- **Issues in Black and White 51**
- **Christianity as Unifier 60**

Why Non-Ethnic Ministers Can Be A Detriment to Ethnic Church? 62
No Race is Perfect or Pure 70
Salvation for Every Nation 74
Diverse Needs of Ministry 76
Hindrances That Prevent Unity 78
Christianity Must Bring Truth 80
Commanded to Witness 91
References 95

Foreword

The nation of America is a very diverse country because of its mixture of people and ideas. It did not recently become diverse because the founding of America was based on a diverse mixture of people, ideas and religious faiths. The European continent from which a majority of its people originated was very similar to the present day make up of this country.

It was inevitable that America would reach a cross road where select groups of people would want to make the nation develop into their particular way of thinking. When the country was weak and busy defending its borders, people had no time for such foolishness. When the people were poor and in need of jobs, people had no time for meddling in another man's business. When media was limited to the local newspaper, the people were limited in how effective they could be in changing the nation within a short period of time.

In the wealth and technological age of current day America, people can push their agendas through media and some without much wealth. However, the rich has always tried to push their agenda on the population because it enhances their bottom line. We are seeing now the clashing of multitudes of ideas and efforts to take over America's destiny.

It was inevitable that it would happen if the moral restraints were moved; and, for certain, they have been moved. Little by little the religious community that has grown larger and larger has gotten quieter and quieter in the community's moral issues, until finally silent. The void which the church has left is quickly being filled up by anyone with a voice.

The church did not leave town, it just decided that it would be satisfied with its wealth and kingdom blessings right down here rather than waiting to get to heaven. In its pursuit to be like everyone else, it has lost its voice and effectiveness. This book looks at the sausage making process to determine what happened and can it be undone.

The Gospel of Jesus Christ has been my rock and neither this writing nor previous ones were written to demean the church. Though necessarily critical at times of some habits by some churches, the books I have written were intended to be an eye opener and warning to the church leaders and its members to show them the danger they were in and spark change. Louder and louder horns have had to be blown to try to awaken the sleeping church. Jesus Christ is coming back for His church -- without spot or wrinkle or any such thing -- and some work will have to be done to get it ready. I am praying continuously for the church.

Joyce Payne

RACIAL VARIATION AND COMPLEXITIES

It has been proven by experts from the science, theological and archeological communities that the population of the world originated on the continent of Africa and that we all come from one gene pool, indicating one family. A report from a 2007 report of the National Geographic News states, "Previous studies have found that genetic differences in human populations can be explained by distance from Africa."(1) A New York Times article states, "All non-Africans are closely related to one another, geneticists found, and they all branch from a family tree rooted in Africa."(2) When we look at the world we live in today we have to wonder how that is possible. The population of the world is so diverse and we seem to have so many cultural variations and so little tolerance or affection for each other's differences. These differences have been the source of wars and great atrocities in our world from mankind's beginning.

The history of the nations and world has evolved over thousands of years and our religious, science and archaeological communities do not agree on how creation commenced or even the age of the earth. Christian authorities cite bible authority and Jewish calculations of the earth's age at about 6,000 years, while the science and archaeological communities argue the earth was formed over several billion years. What we do know for sure is that changes have occurred at every level to make us a diverse people. Wars and transcontinental marriages change the face of territories over time as new races and nations are formed from those interactions. Also formed from those relationships are new faiths and beliefs that deviate from that first taught and have resulted in many religions and practices that now frame the thought and actions of the world's population.

ETHNICITY IN OUR COMMUNITIES

Our world today is a multi-ethnic world consisting of people from various backgrounds who reside in groups based on their particular nation, culture, heritage, language, tradition or race. This variation came about because of disobedience but residing with people where there is a common language may also be a necessity for survival. Communities are often established based on similarities as people interact in an environment that allows them to share their lives with others of like interest in their social setting.

Ethnicity is a word that we use to refer to the state of a group of people belonging to a region or social group where they share in common heritage, beliefs, language or traditions among themselves. Ethnic groups have names or titles that identify their particular grouping. An ethnic group is identified as a population considered as a subgroup of the more dominant grouping of people residing in the area with a different set of values and traditions. The ideas and special behavior of a people represents their culture. Some of the differences that may distinguish one culture from another are speech, dance, clothing style, type housing, parenting techniques, diet, physical appearance, religion or commerce. The designation of an ethnic group and their name can sometimes reveal a bias from the dominant community toward the subgroup. America is made up of many cultures with vast differences who are all referred to as Americans even though they are also recognized as subgroups of a dominate class of people who themselves established this nation as European immigrants.

The continent of Europe is composed of many countries with cultures varying from those of their neighboring lands. Europe has gone through many evolutions because it has been a land conquered and settled by many warring forces. The English, French, Italians, Swedes and other nations all live in Europe but have cultural traditions, language and foods completely different from their neighbors, denoting their influence or history. The continent of Africa, as well, is made up of many nations and immigrants with various cultures from their native land. People living in America who originated from Mexico have a culture different than those residing in America originating from China. Some cities in America have neighborhoods based on cultural traditions such as those designated as "China Town", where Chinese commerce is emphasized. Some cities are even divided by gang designation. The culture of a group of people may be distinguished by their social or religious traditions (e.g. Amish Community, Catholic convents or monasteries). Where cultures intersect, it can cause the mixing of ideals, where compromises are made; or it can cause a culture clash, where people refuse any change to their long-standing traditions.

The biblical Jews living during the Roman occupation would have been an ethnic group of the Roman Empire and their Jewish traditions represented a different cultural life. The Jews were easily recognizable from the Romans by wearing apparel and language. Their ethnicity clashed with that of the Romans but did not present a serious threat to the powerful Roman government because of Rome's superior power. The Jewish culture pertained mostly to their religious rites, which were of no consequence to the Romans as long as it did not usurp their authority. However, talk of a king superior of Caesar did spark their interest.

America was formed as a nation from many different ethnic people from Europe that traveled to the new land as pilgrims after the 1492 land discovery. The land was already occupied by a people the pilgrims called "Indians" who were eventually defeated or relocated to Indian reservations. The pilgrims, coming from various European countries, continued their own traditions, religious rites and social customs but united as a people in America to colonize the new land. The settlers prospered because their varied cultures, sometimes divided by states, were formed into a larger society where they respected each other's varied cultures and united in national identification as Americans. The nation of America today is made up of many subgroups. The largest grouping we identify as "whites" are actually the people who have their cultural heritage from many European countries before coming to America. Many white Americans identify their family heritage as Italian, German, Sweden, Irish, French, British, etc., while other citizens have their heritage in parts of Asia, Africa, Mexico or the Islands.

Some of the subgroups in America divided by religion and social culture are Mormon, Jew, Muslim, Buddhist, Catholic, Amish, Native Americans, etc. The Pew Research Center performs survey on American society and identifies religious groups by race and their percentage of the population. Christians of many Protestant denominations still make up the largest religious population of America from early pioneering days. The Pew Research study in 2014 listed in America a 70.6 percent Christian population for adults. Christian America continues to reach new converts as they utilize the modern advantages of major television networks and media to propagate the message of Jesus Christ.

DIVERSITIES CAME BECAUSE OF UNIFIED EVIL

When the known world had just one language, the people united together and set out to usurp the authority of God. The biblical account is known as the story of the Tower of Babel in Nimrod's kingdom (Gen. 10:9; 11:1-9). Their united front and effort to build a city with a tower that would reach unto heaven and prevent them from being disbursed across the earth was spoiled by the God of heaven who saw the wickedness of man's mind. God said that through their unity nothing would restrain them from what they imagined to do. He came down to stop their plans by confounding their language that caused them to scatter to all corners of the earth.

ESTABLISHMENT OF CHRISTIAN RELIGION

From the wicked condition of the earth, God saw a man named Abram (later changed to Abraham) from whom He promised to build a holy nation that would bring the world back to righteousness. The nation was called Israel and from Abraham's seed would come the promised Messiah and Savior of the world, Jesus Christ. This covenant of salvation and blessings between God and man is still in force and is propagated through the Christian faith.

Though it is not the oldest religion, Christianity has been the most enduring of faiths and alone can trace its origin back to the beginning of the earth and man's faith in God. The bible is the Christian's instruction book given by God and it is still the world's best-selling book. Its author is the Creator of all things, who lives in eternity and who alone was present at creation and is able to describe the origin of man and the earth. Mankind through ignorance has claimed many gods but Jehovah God alone supersedes and disproves every other deity.

The Christian religion owes it origin to the faith of Patriarch Abraham and his Jewish descendants. Though the Jewish religion and its people have undergone many wars, disbursement, persecutions, and assimilations; the faith has survived intact by God's providence for our generation and those to come. The bible, which is written history for Jews and Christian believers, contains the Word of God given from the hands of 40 divinely-inspired writers over a span of 1500 years and whose accounts all stand in agreement in purpose and content. The written accounts have been validated by modern archeological discoveries of bible texts such as the Dead Sea Scrolls found in a cave by the Judean desert in 1947 and subsequent archeological and DNA evidence from over 2,000 years ago.

With all the evidence of Christian authenticity, miracles and multitudes of world-wide believers; the religion is still under attack by unbelieving scientists, atheists, other religions and some apostate Christians. When Christianity is practiced according to the faith of the first believers, who set strong examples for us to follow, we arrive at the same miraculous results and faith as they experienced. We are not expected to improve on the gospel but rather to follow it for the same results as the first church. Our Christian churches are a continuation of their faith and is destined to change from glory to glory until we reach like experience as Enoch (Gen. 5:24) or Elijah (II Ki 2:11) who were taken bodily up into heaven. It is when we think that we are better than they and must do things different than they, that we are led into false religions that yield idolatrous worshippers.

CHRISTIAN GOSPEL FIRST DIRECTED TO ETHNIC COMMUNITY

Evangelism

Our bible tells us that God scattered the population of the world and He is well able to heal and bring the world's people together again to a godly unity. That is the goal of the gospel message. He ordained a plan for restoration before the foundation of the world. He instituted His plan first by using men to help save man. Abraham was appointed to bring into the earth a family of priests who would draw the world back to God. Abraham was faithful but the weakness of mankind prevented this solution. God utilized His only begotten Son, Jesus the Christ, to come to earth and save man. Christianity is the story of God's efforts to save mankind. The church is His instrument to bring forth His plan.

The church has been given everything it needs to accomplish this goal: guidance and power from God, leaders to instruct and people to assist. Our world is witnessing and watching how the church carries out this assignment. Our world is violently screaming out that the church has failed in its responsibility to fulfill God's will. So while we still have time, let's evaluate the instructions God gave the church.

Besides regular church preaching services a popular method of delivering the message of Jesus Christ in modern American society is evangelism. Evangelism is often performed through preachers who go out into the population to dissimilate the message of Christ to a worldly population to bring them to Christ. Jesus told Peter and Andrew upon meeting them that He would make them fishers of men. In the early years of America, circuit preachers and evangelists rode through the land preaching the gospel to the saved and unsaved. Churches sprung up from these evangelistic services and pastors were appointed. Churches today call evangelism a service where a preacher from another church comes to their local assembly. The messages are primarily to the saved and the object of the service has become one of revival or fundraising. Churches also sponsor overseas campaigns to "evangelize" the unsaved in foreign nations. Another popular method of evangelism is performed by the laity where they form teams to do "cold witnessing" for Christ. These believers go out together to witness salvation to anyone on the streets regardless of age, gender, background or religion. Their scriptural support for this method is words by Jesus. We read in Mark 16:15 that Jesus "said unto them, Go ye into all the world, and preach the gospel to every creature." The teaching of Christianity is that Jesus Christ accepts all people regardless of gender, culture or race. Christians are taught in church that cold witnessing is an evangelistic way to share the gospel and reach the lost of the world. So the scriptures and practice seem to validate this practice of witnessing. But is this really what Jesus taught? Did he really intend for every new born-again believer to go witnessing cold turkey?

How Did Jesus Teach Witnessing?

> And that repentance and remission of sins should be preached in his name among all nations, <u>beginning at Jerusalem</u>. Luk 24:47

> But ye shall receive power, after that the Holy Ghost is come upon you: and ye shall be witnesses unto me both in <u>Jerusalem</u>, and in all Judaea, and in Samaria, and unto the uttermost part of the earth. Act 1:8

> Unto <u>you first</u> God, having raised up his Son Jesus, sent him to bless you, in turning away every one of you from his iniquities. Acts 3:26

> These twelve Jesus sent forth, and commanded them, saying, Go not into the way of the Gentiles, and into any city of the Samaritans enter ye not: Mat 10:6 But <u>go rather to the lost sheep of the house of Israel</u>. Mat 10:5

> Now I say that Jesus Christ was a minister of the circumcision for the truth of God, to confirm the promises made unto the fathers: Rom 15:8

The scriptures above show the direction Jesus preferred for His disciples to go witness and it was to lost people of the Jewish faith first before witnessing to people of other nations. In fact, He specifically said in His instructions to His 12 disciples in Matthew 10:5 that they should not go to the Gentile or non-Israelite nations.

Why We Misunderstood What Jesus Taught?

Our purpose here is to understand why Christ gave those instructions and how it should impact our witnessing efforts. The Old Testament taught that we should not just casually read scripture but rather seek wisdom and strive to get understanding. Understanding is obtained through studying and comparing bible scripture that interprets itself to extract the intent and purpose of what is said.

> Whom shall he teach knowledge? and whom shall he make to understand doctrine?...For precept must be upon precept, precept upon precept; line upon line, line upon line; here a little, and there a little…Isa 28:9-10

> Wisdom is the principal thing; therefore get wisdom: and with all thy getting get understanding. Pro 4:7

The teachings of the New Testament substantiate that we must search scripture and study parallel scriptures in other chapters or books to get correct understanding:

> Search the scriptures; for in them ye think ye have eternal life: and they are they which testify of me. Joh 5:39

> All scripture is given by inspiration of God, and is

> profitable for doctrine, for reproof, for correction, for instruction in righteousness…2Ti 3:16

> And he said unto them, Know ye not this parable? and how then will ye know all parables? Mar 4:13

> And with many such parables spake he the word unto them, as they were able to hear it. But without a parable spake he not unto them: and when they were alone, he expounded all things to his disciples. Mar 4:33-34

> Study to shew thyself approved unto God, a workman that needeth not to be ashamed, rightly dividing the word of truth. 2Ti 2:15

So we are taught to not just take a scripture at face value but to study the whole of scriptures for true meaning and to obtain its wisdom. We must consider the setting, the speaker, audience, time and purpose of the text. Wisdom is derived by comparing scripture with scripture to obtain understanding like the wisdom gained when the Old Testament interprets, demonstrates or explains the New Testament or vice versa. The best understanding of what Jesus intended by the Mark 16:15 command to His disciples is what He actually said and demonstrated.

Old and New Testament Scripture Reveal Recipient of the Message

> Old Testament
>
> Rejoice greatly, O daughter of Zion; shout, O daughter of Jerusalem: behold, thy King cometh unto thee: he is just, and having salvation; lowly, and riding upon an ass, and upon a colt the foal of an ass. Zec 9:9

> Hear this word that the LORD hath spoken against you, O children of Israel, against the whole family

which I brought up from the land of Egypt, saying, You only have I known of all the families of the earth: therefore I will punish you for all your iniquities. Amos 3:1-2

New Testament

He came unto his own, and his own received him not. Joh 1:11

And he taught daily in the temple. But the chief priests and the scribes and the chief of the people sought to destroy him…Luk 19:47

These twelve Jesus sent forth, and commanded them, saying, Go not into the way of the Gentiles, and into any city of the Samaritans enter ye not: But go rather to the lost sheep of the house of Israel. And as ye go, preach, saying, The kingdom of heaven is at hand. Mat 10:5-7

And it came to pass, when Jesus had made an end of commanding his twelve disciples, he departed thence to teach and to preach in their cities. Mat 11:1

Afterward he appeared unto the eleven as they sat at meat, and upbraided them with their unbelief and hardness of heart, because they believed not them which had seen him after he was risen. And he said unto them, Go ye into all the world, and preach the gospel to every creature. He that believeth and is baptized shall be saved; but he that believeth not shall be damned. Mar 16:14-16

The scriptures above reveal that Jesus came first to the Jewish people and sent His disciples to teach their own ethnic group of Jews as He had done. But after teaching and instructing His people, being rejected and crucified by them, He later directs them to preach to the Gentile world. One scripture says that He went unto His own which means He went to those of His own ethnicity, the Jewish people. Those that he recruited for his 12 disciples and fellow ministers were all Jews and they were sent to preach only to the Jews at first. In

Matthew 10:5-7 Jesus specifically commanded the disciples not to go to the non-Jew population, but rather to the Jewish nation alone.

WHY JESUS ORIGINALLY LIMITED HIS MESSAGE TO HIS OWN PEOPLE

The bible started out with God speaking to one man, Adam, and his wife, Eve, who were to be the first family populating the earth with godly children as the family of God. Sin entered into the first family and they became disinherited and lost to God as a family. The Old Testament rehearses the story of God trying to recover His covenant family and restore them back into loving relationship with Him. It is important to note here that God is restoring "family" and that His first creation was "family".

> Rejoice greatly, O daughter of Zion; shout, O daughter of Jerusalem: behold, thy King cometh unto thee: he is just, and having salvation [deliverance from sin and its consequences*]; lowly, and riding upon an ass, and upon a colt the foal of an ass. Zec 9:9

> Now when Jesus was born in Bethlehem of Judaea in the days of Herod the king, behold, there came wise men from the east to Jerusalem, Saying, Where is he that is born King of the Jews [a deliverer and ruler to reign over the disbursed people]? for we have seen his star in the east, and are come to worship him. Mat 2:1-2 [* Author's notation]

> O Jerusalem, Jerusalem, thou that killest the prophets, and stonest them which are sent unto thee, how often would I have gathered thy children together, even as a hen gathereth her

> chickens under her wings, and ye would not! Mat 23:37

The scriptures above refer to a King of the Jews, not to the gentiles or the world but King to the Jews alone. The scriptures reveal that this was their king coming to His own people. The Old Testament record God's many efforts through signs and wonders, prophetic voices and dire consequences to draw His wayward children back to obedience and relationship with Him for their own survival and blessings. The Old Testament prophets wrote of the birth of Jesus as the fulfillment of God's covenant promise to His covenant people. We can note here as well that the New Testament is really love letters written to Christ's family, bride or church.

Abrahamic Covenant Fulfilled

God seeks to save every man but His call for mankind to trust Him was received by Abram, a man who found favor with God. He was a man who was able to lead his whole household back to God. In return, God made a covenant with Abraham that his descendants would be a special people set aside to fulfill His purpose in the earth. His family was to be a royal priesthood for God to all the people of the earth. The Old Testament scripture details God's dealings with Abraham's descendants in obedience and in disobedience after they walked away from Him. God then gave them the Law through the Abrahamic descendant named Moses, who would teach the people ways of faithfulness. The Law also failed to bring these descendants, later called Children of Israel, into obedience. However, a promise was made to a faithful Abrahamic descendant named King David that his seed would inherit an eternal throne. David was the beloved King of the Israelite nation, and though his kingdom was later destroyed, the Jews longed for its rebuilding.

> Then will I stablish the throne of thy kingdom, according as I have covenanted with David thy father, saying, There shall not fail thee a man to be ruler in Israel. 2 Ch 7:18

The descendants of Abraham and David were Israelites with the same bloodline and religious beliefs. The last known tribes of the original Children of Israel were descendants of the tribe of Judah, called Jews, who continued many of their traditions in remote places where they fled. It was prophesied in the Old Testament that a Deliverer/Messiah would come unto the Children of Israel from the Davidic line who would reestablished the kingdom of David for the Jews. It was not long after the coming of Christ, the Son of David, to Jerusalem in the midst of their Roman bondage that the disciples of Jesus asked whether or not now the kingdom would be restored. They looked for the physical throne and kingdom to be restored but Christ came instead to bring about the reign of a spiritual King and establish a spiritual kingdom that would reign in earth and heaven for eternity. Christ was born as a man and in the human lineage and bloodline of Abraham and King David. His mission as the Jewish Messiah was to fulfill the Law, provide forgiveness and salvation for the lost family of God, fulfill the promise of an eternal kingdom for David and restore the land of Israel to Abraham's descendants.

> And Moses went up unto God, and the LORD called unto him out of the mountain, saying, Thus shalt thou say to the house of Jacob, and tell the children of Israel; Ye have seen what I did unto the Egyptians, and how I bare you on eagles' wings, and brought you unto myself. Now therefore, if ye will obey my voice indeed, and keep my covenant, then ye shall be <u>a peculiar treasure unto me above all people</u>: for all the earth is mine: And <u>ye shall be unto me a kingdom of priests</u>, and an holy nation. These are the words which thou shalt speak unto the children of Israel. Exo 19:3-6
>
> <u>He also exalteth the horn of his people</u>, the praise of all his saints; even of the children of Israel, a <u>people near unto him</u>. Praise ye the LORD. Psa 148:14

God purposed to have a faithful people who would be royal priests to minister to the rest of the world. Israel was set aside to be that royal priesthood to all other nations. We find that the gospel of Matthew is an account of the coming of the prophesied Messiah/King. Matthew is a book with a message written from Jews to the Jews about their Jewish King coming to deliver His own people from bondage. He first called this people to Himself and then taught them the percepts and ways of their God. After learning God's ways and becoming examples of faithful living and obedience to God, they were to be priesthood to their own people first and then draw other nations into God's sheep-fold.

> And other sheep I have, which are not of this fold: them also I must bring, and they shall hear my voice; and there shall be one fold, and one shepherd. Joh 10:16
>
> But ye are a chosen generation, a royal priesthood, an holy nation, a peculiar people; that ye should shew forth the praises of him who hath called you out of darkness into his marvellous light… 1Pe 2:9

So the example set forth for the people of Israel and subsequently for the church is that God saves us as witnesses at home first and then He sends us out as examples of His love to witness to the outside world and draw them into His kingdom. We reach those in our ethnic or cultural circles first before reaching out to the world. Jesus demonstrated this by witnessing to His own people first before reaching out to the world and instructed His disciples to follow His example. He was the long awaited Jewish Messiah coming to deliver his family, the Israelite nation.

He came unto his own, and his own received him not. Joh 1:11

Imagine what might have happened if the Jews were first sent out to witness to the Romans or even to the Greeks before witnessing to their own friends and family? The Romans were their mortal enemies and had no reason to trust a testimony of the rising from the dead one they had crucified. The Jews often had to hide among friends or family to prevent persecution or death at Roman hands. They had no witnessing power with the Romans.

The problem God had with the nation of Israel in the wilderness was that He could not get them to remain faithful to learn His ways, live out the example in truth and become priests to a hostile world. Israel continually rebelled and sinned, disqualifying for service as priests to the world. The mission and message of Jesus was to provide a means for them to return to the Father's bosom and finish their destiny as a family of priests with holy power supplied by God to reach the rest of the world with the gospel message. Jesus was first trained and approved among His own people before being approved by God for leadership to others. He was brought up in the Jewish traditions under the Law and validated through John, the Baptist's ministry as the Lamb of God sent by the Father.

> The next day John seeth Jesus coming unto him, and saith, Behold the Lamb of God, which taketh away the sin of the world. This is he of whom I said, After me cometh a man which is preferred before me: for he was before me. Joh 1:29-30

> And I saw, and bare record that this is the Son of God. Joh 1:34

The bible tells us the word should be established by two or three witnesses. After the witness of John that Jesus was the long-awaited Messiah for the Jews, the Father gave His witness from heaven:

> Now when all the people were baptized, it came to pass, that Jesus also being baptized, and praying, the heaven was opened, And the Holy Ghost descended in a bodily shape like a dove upon him, and a voice came from heaven, which said, Thou art my beloved Son; in thee I am well pleased. Luk 3:21-22

> While he thus spake, there came a cloud, and overshadowed them: and they feared as they

> entered into the cloud. And there came a voice out of the cloud, saying, This is my beloved Son: hear him. Luk 9:34 -35

Jesus already had a good reputation among His own people and was acceptable in the Jewish faith. He received the witness of John, the Word of God, His ministry of miracles, as well as by Peter and other disciples. He was accepted by man and God.

After His crucifixion and ascension to heaven, Jesus sent the Holy Spirit, to live inside the disciples, providing power to live holy. The obedient followers of Christ were then to deliver the message of hope and salvation to the world, eventually bringing all people into the sheepfold. So God was looking for a family of ministers to serve as His emissaries in the earth. Their example is a lesson for us today. God is still calling the faithful to Himself for instruction and assignment as a holy priesthood. Jesus taught His disciples to follow His example and His example was one of being proven in the home environment and by God before going to witness to the world. The disciples followed His example and they taught we should follow Jesus through their footsteps.

> And other sheep I have, which are not of this fold: them also I must bring, and they shall hear my voice; and there shall be one fold, and one shepherd. Joh 10:16

Notice in the above scripture that Jesus has one group in the fold then adds other. He stated there were other people from a different "fold" that would join in with them, all having one shepherd (Himself) over them. Paul told the Corinthians, "Let all things be done decently and in order." He often spoke of setting things "in order" (Acts 18:23, I Cor. 11:34, 15:23). In the Old Testament particularly, we see that God specifies order and set times and seasons for His work.

Requirement of Faithfulness

The lesson that some people may miss is that they must first possess a perfected life or walk with God before qualifying to teach others. The word perfected refers to mature rather than one having no fault. We work toward deliverance from sin throughout life. Even Jesus is reported to have learned obedience through the things He suffered. Paul taught us about striving to keep his body under submission. The standard of holiness for a minister mirrors the Old Testament practice of the Levites' required cleansing before service in the tabernacle (Num. 8:5-22). Jesus had personally taught his disciples the way to be effective in their witness for Him.

> Ye are the salt of the earth: but if the salt have lost his savour, wherewith shall it be salted? it is thenceforth good for nothing, but to be cast out, and to be trodden under foot of men. Ye are the light of the world. A city that is set on an hill cannot be hid. Neither do men light a candle, and put it under a bushel, but on a candlestick; and it giveth light unto all that are in the house. Let your light so shine before men, that they may see your good works, and glorify your Father which is in heaven. Mat 5:13-16

> Be ye therefore perfect, even as your Father which is in heaven is perfect. Mat 5:48

> The disciple is not above his master: but every one that is perfect shall be as his master. Luk 6:40

> Wherefore lay apart all filthiness and superfluity of naughtiness, and receive with meekness the engrafted word, which is able to save your souls. But be ye doers of the word, and not hearers only, deceiving your own selves. For if any be a hearer of the word, and not a doer, he is like unto a man beholding his natural face in a glass…Jas 1:21-23

> And let these also first be proved; then let them use the office of a deacon, being found blameless. Even so must their wives be grave, not slanderers, sober, faithful in all things. Let the deacons be the husbands of one wife, ruling their children and their own houses well. 1Ti 3:10-12

> And for their sakes I sanctify myself, that they also might be sanctified through the truth. Joh 17:19

Jesus taught His disciples to be lights of the world that others could see. He was referring to their being a witness and a preserver of right in their communities. James' gospel further brought out the message that men must be a doer of the word and not just a hearer. So they had to constantly work to keep themselves clean and doing what was right. Jesus intended that men would teach what they were themselves living. This is illustrated in His prayer to the Father (Jo 17:10) that He sanctified himself so that those He preached to could be sanctified by the word He preached. Paul taught: "Brethren, be followers together of me, and mark them which walk so as ye have us for an ensample (Php 3:17)." He taught: in 1Ti 3:7 "Moreover he must have a good report of them which are without; lest he fall into reproach and the snare of the devil." After living out their faith and teaching in their own proving ground of home and community, they were next to reach out further and be a witness to all the world as Jesus later instructed His disciples.

> And he said unto them, Go ye into all the world, and preach the gospel to every creature. He that believeth and is baptized shall be saved; but he that believeth not shall be damned. Mar 16:15-16

The pattern is set in both the Old and New Testaments for the church to imitate but often the church finds it own way to do things as did the tribe of Israel. Jesus taught the example of witnessing in our home, neighborhood, and then going abroad. Witnessing in our own environment prepares us, the soil for fruit-bearing and gives us a more sanctified environment that we find rest in. Jesus, as God in the flesh, walked out the right steps of ministry to supply us a perfect example to follow.

> But ye shall receive power, after that the Holy Ghost is come upon you: and ye shall be witnesses unto me both in Jerusalem, and in all Judaea, and in Samaria, and unto the uttermost part of the earth. Act 1:8

Jesus, as God in the flesh and Savior of the world, spent 30 years as a flesh man before taking on His role in ministry as Savior. He was just as much God as a baby as He was when an adult. But scripture shows us His pattern of growing and maturing into a physical man and learning obedience under parents and community authorities through the things He suffered (Heb 5:8). Jesus went through this process of growing naturally and developing into ministry as an example for us. The Old Testament taught that men were to be proven to be honorable at home and in the community before being established as leaders among their people. Their daily lives were to be witnessed as honorable. This was a protection for the one being established as leader and the people. The most honorable people being those faithful to God could then be selected as leaders in both church and society to bring glory to God and blessings to the people. Notice here that even social, business and political leaders were to be honorable men.

> Moreover thou shalt provide out of all the people able men, such as fear God, men of truth, hating covetousness; and place such over them, to be rulers of thousands, and rulers of hundreds, rulers of fifties, and rulers of tens: Exo 18:21

> Wherefore, brethren, look ye out among you seven men of honest report, full of the Holy Ghost and wisdom, whom we may appoint over this business. Act 6:3

> This is a true saying, If a man desire the office of a bishop, he desireth a good work. A bishop then must be blameless, the husband of one wife, vigilant, sober, of good behaviour, given to hospitality, apt to teach; Not given to wine, no striker, not greedy of filthy lucre; but patient, not a brawler, not covetous; One that ruleth well his own house, having his children in subjection with all gravity; (For if a man know not how to rule his own house, how shall he take care of the church of God?) Not a novice, lest being lifted up with pride he fall into the condemnation of the devil. Moreover he must have a good report of them which are without; lest he fall into reproach and the snare of the devil. Likewise must the deacons be grave, not doubletongued, not given to much wine, not greedy of filthy lucre; Holding the mystery of the faith in a pure conscience. And let these also first be proved; then let them use the office of a deacon, being found blameless. 1Ti 3:1-10

The scriptures above clearly state that those serving in the church office from deacon to bishop must be people who have their own house in check and have proven themselves faithful and able to control those under their own authority before assuming authority over others. This method of choosing honorable men would preserve our society. Jesus was our perfect example for faithfulness. He said He only did those things He saw His Father do. He showed obedience to His mother and provided for her needs through the miracle of the wine and appointment of John to care for His mother at the crucifixion. God, the Father, gave His approval over all that Jesus did.

> For he received from God the Father honour and glory, when there came such a voice to him from the excellent glory, This is my beloved Son, in whom I am well pleased. 2Pe 1:17

The modern church is experiencing problems that stem from not following the above scripture where proven godly men were to carry out leadership positions. It was only after a person had proven he was faithful in the presence of his family, community and church that he could be set up as a leader over the people in any capacity in the church or society. It is clear to most of us in church today that this practice is not being followed and churches often bring in leaders from other cities where their lifestyles cannot possibly be observed, proven or evaluated by the church congregation before installation to church office. Also popular today is the practice of bringing in unknown speakers from other regions and the "celebrity preacher" whose life is lived in gated or sheltered communities where people cannot know, evaluate or judge any ungodly behavior.

Requirement of Identification

The purpose of identification is another reason why Christianity is first directed to ethnicity or people of one's own culture. We know that God revealed Himself as Christ and that God put on a body of flesh and dwelt among His chosen people to live and suffer as they did. Then as one of them He chose to be sacrificed for them and bare their punishment to satisfy the Father's wrath. Christ identified with the people He came to witness to and save. Jesus began to preach and to say, repent for the kingdom of heaven is at hand (Mt 4:17). His message revealed who He was: a Jewish Messenger; that He was sent to Jews looking for restoration of David's kingdom; and His message was that the Kingdom is here. Everything about His message was directed to His own people who looked for the promise. He was connecting with their history and revealing their path forward. He did not have to take time to prove who He was or His authority to speak to them because He was one of them. He had lived among them, was respected among them, had learned and taught in their temple and had worked miracles among them.

> Forasmuch then as the children are partakers of flesh and blood, he also himself likewise took part of the same; that through death he might destroy him that had the power of death, that is, the devil; And deliver them who through fear of death were all their lifetime subject to bondage. For

> verily he took not on him the nature of angels; but he took on him the seed of Abraham. Wherefore in all things it behoved him to be made like unto his brethren, that he might be a merciful and faithful high priest in things pertaining to God, to make reconciliation for the sins of the people. For in that he himself hath suffered being tempted, he is able to succour them that are tempted. Heb 2:14-18

> He came unto his own, and his own received him not. Joh 1:11

Christian instruction from our Lord was that we were to follow Him so we follow the example He left on record and do as He did and like His apostles did. Our witness must also be first directed to our own people in our own homes and community before it is shared with other regions. First of all, our training ground is at home in our own environment. If we can win our own family, our Christian experience will be made that much easier. Family can be the hardest people to win; but once won, they are a powerful witness for us. But if we do not perfect a Christian walk at home and have witness for our profession of holiness, there is no validation for ministry. Our day-to-day life must be our first witness. Our qualification to minister is that we possess and have proven a good report at home and in the community. The minister must be blameless at home lest being lifted up with pride he falls into the condemnation of the devil. Condemnation will always come from the devil; but when it is found false, it will fail. However, condemnation found to be true will surely bring with it an eminent fall.

> My manner of life from my youth, which was at the first among mine own nation at Jerusalem, know all the Jews; Which knew me from the beginning, if they would testify, that after the most straitest sect of our religion I lived a Pharisee. Act 26:4-5

> Are they Hebrews? so am I. Are they Israelites? so am I. Are they the seed of Abraham? so am I. Are

> they ministers of Christ? (I speak as a fool) I am more; in labours more abundant, in stripes above measure, in prisons more frequent, in deaths oft. 2Co 11:22-23

> Fight the good fight of faith, lay hold on eternal life, whereunto thou art also called, and hast professed a good profession before many witnesses. 1Ti 6:12

In the scriptures above, we have Apostle Paul's witness and testimony about his status as a Jewish minister living before his peers. A minister should be first known in his own home before he is released to minister in the world. This is the practice that Christ, Himself, followed. He ministered in His Jewish culture, where he was evaluated, tested, tried and proven. As mentioned before, Christ's approval came from the only one who could evaluate Him: God, the Father. His disciples not only watched and observed His life but witnessed that He was the Savior. After the 12 Jewish disciples were trained and approved by Jesus, they were released from their initial ministry to the Jews to go into all the world and preach the gospel to all men. Actually it was Paul who received the ministry to the gentiles. The presentation of the gospel to the gentiles had been prohibited to all the apostles until Christ released and commissioned Peter first to witness outside the faith to the gentiles. Paul later confirmed that his ministry was to go to the gentiles after first sharing with and trying to persuade the Jews.

> For I am not ashamed of the gospel of Christ: for it is the power of God unto salvation to every one that believeth; to the Jew first, and also to the Greek. Rom 1:16

We see the ministry in early days being given to an African eunuch as it was also given in tongues to all nations at Pentecost. The Old Testament prophesied that the gospel would be shared with the gentiles and even Christ taught the gentile woman at the well in Samaria, who also bore witness to Jesus that the Jews would have nothing to do with other nations. The focus of ministry is directed first to one's own people and then to others as Jesus taught. Timothy later taught a principle that is generally accepted by all as true:

> But if any provide not for his own, and specially for those of his own house, he hath denied the faith, and is worse than an infidel. 1Ti 5:8

Our first service, after devotion to God, is to our own family. The extended family would be relatives, friends and the community. We have an obligation to those that support us and should show support back to them. We are part of a larger family in our neighborhood and cultural family. Upon salvation, God cleanses us but He also starts cleaning around us in our environment, making a better life for us. If He did not work on our environment as well, everyday life would be unbearable for a sanctified child of God. Lot was contaminated in an immoral city "vexed with the filthy conversation of the wicked (2Pe 2:7)."

Qualification for Priesthood

Out of the twelve tribes of Israel, God arranged for the Levites tribe to serve as priesthood for the nation of Israel forever. Their service was to God on behalf of the people. They had special privileges of provision for their needs from the people but also had special requirements of sanctification for the office of priest.

> And thou shalt anoint them, as thou didst anoint their father, that they may minister unto me in the priest's office: for their anointing shall surely be an everlasting priesthood throughout their generations. Exo 40:15

God sought to use the children of Israel for the work of earthly priesthood throughout their generations but they failed the qualification of faithfulness.

> Remember them, O my God, because they have defiled the priesthood, and the covenant of the priesthood, and of the Levites. Neh 13:29

The unfaithfulness of the Levites for priesthood caused God to take the office from the tribe of Levites. Jesus came as the perfect priest, not of the tribe of Levi, from the tribe of Judah.

> If therefore perfection were by the Levitical priesthood, (for under it the people received the law,) what further need was there that another priest should rise after the order of Melchisedec, and not be called after the order of Aaron? For the priesthood being changed, there is made of necessity a change also of the law. For he of whom these things are spoken pertaineth to another tribe, of which no man gave attendance at the altar. For it is evident that our Lord sprang out of Juda; of which tribe Moses spake nothing concerning priesthood. Heb 7:11-14

The Jews missed their last opportunity to be set up as priesthood when they rejected their Messiah and the opportunity to be restored through Jesus.

> O Jerusalem, Jerusalem, thou that killest the prophets, and stonest them which are sent unto thee, how often would I have gathered thy children together, even as a hen gathereth her chickens under her wings, and ye would not! Behold, your house is left unto you desolate. For I say unto you, Ye shall not see me henceforth, till ye shall say, Blessed is he that cometh in the name of the Lord. Mat 23:37-39

Their rejection of their Messiah opened the door for the gentiles to be accepted into the plan of salvation. Jesus came to establish an earthly priesthood that would be responsible for ministering the message of salvation to the lost, poor, oppressed and afflicted everywhere. Jesus came under the Law, was faithful to the Father as a substitute for our failure and now has made available to every believer and nation of humans the opportunity to serve the Father in priesthood to the world.

> Ye also, as lively stones, are built up a spiritual house, an holy priesthood, to offer up spiritual sacrifices, acceptable to God by Jesus Christ. Wherefore also it is contained in the scripture, Behold, I lay in Sion a chief corner stone, elect, precious: and he that believeth on him shall not be confounded. 1Pe 2:5-6

Christ's death makes every believer a part of the priesthood for the purpose of bringing souls to Christ. This is a part of the Christian's everyday life as he lives for Christ. There is a difference, however, between the requirement of laity and those that have special callings as clergy to the body of Christ. Those established in formal ministry in the church to witness as church leaders to the body of Christ are listed in the book of Ephesians and, like the Levitical priesthood, they have specific responsibilities and requirements for those offices.

> He that descended is the same also that ascended up far above all heavens, that he might fill all things.) And he gave some, apostles; and some, prophets; and some, evangelists; and some, pastors and teachers; For the perfecting of the saints, for the work of the ministry, for the edifying of the body of Christ…Eph 4:10 -12

> This is a true saying, If a man desire the office of a bishop, he desireth a good work. A bishop then must be blameless, the husband of one wife, vigilant, sober, of good behaviour, given to hospitality, apt to teach; Not given to wine, no striker, not greedy of filthy lucre; but patient, not a brawler, not covetous; One that ruleth well his own house, having his children in subjection with all gravity; (For if a man know not how to rule his own house, how shall he take care of the church of God?

> 6 Not a novice, lest being lifted up with pride he fall into the condemnation of the devil. Moreover he must have a good report of them which are without; lest he fall into reproach and the snare of the devil. 8 Likewise must the deacons be grave, not doubletongued, not given to much wine, not greedy of filthy lucre; Holding the mystery of the faith in a pure conscience. And let these also first be proved; then let them use the office of a deacon, being found blameless. Even so must their wives be grave, not slanderers, sober, faithful in all things. Let the deacons be the husbands of one wife, ruling their children and their own houses well. For they that have used the office of a deacon well purchase to themselves a good degree, and great boldness in the faith which is in Christ Jesus. I Tim 3:1-13

In the New Testament, every believer is an heir of Jesus, adopted in the family and is part of the priesthood. The message of Christ is to be dispersed through the personal ministry of every believer. The church ministry and outreach team evangelizes the world from the ordained leadership in the church. Both the Christian congregation and the leadership are expected to live a life of holiness empowered by the Holy Spirit to be living epistles or witnesses to the world. We are witness to those we encounter daily. Scripture illustrates that it is Christ or the Holy Spirit who direct disciples into world outreach.

> But ye shall receive power, after that the Holy Ghost is come upon you: and ye shall be witnesses unto me both in Jerusalem, and in all Judaea, and in Samaria, and unto the uttermost part of the earth. Act 1:8

> Now when they had gone throughout Phrygia and the region of Galatia, and were <u>forbidden of the</u>

> Holy Ghost to preach the word in Asia, After they were come to Mysia, they assayed to go into Bithynia: but the Spirit suffered them not. Act 16:6-7

> And the angel of the Lord spake unto Philip, saying, Arise, and go toward the south unto the way that goeth down from Jerusalem unto Gaza, which is desert. And he arose and went: and, behold, a man of Ethiopia, an eunuch of great authority under Candace queen of the Ethiopians, who had the charge of all her treasure, and had come to Jerusalem for to worship, Was returning, and sitting in his chariot read Esaias the prophet. Then the Spirit said unto Philip, Go near, and join thyself to this chariot. Act 8:26-29

> Now there were in the church that was at Antioch certain prophets and teachers; as Barnabas, and Simeon that was called Niger, and Lucius of Cyrene, and Manaen, which had been brought up with Herod the tetrarch, and Saul. As they ministered to the Lord, and fasted, the Holy Ghost said, Separate me Barnabas and Saul for the work whereunto I have called them. And when they had fasted and prayed, and laid their hands on them, they sent them away. Act 13:1-3

Jesus showed us through His life that He followed the direction of the Father and sought the Father's direction for His work. It is Jesus who is in control of His ministry and He leads us into witnessing as led by the Holy Spirit. If we follow the leadings of the Holy Spirit, we will know when to speak, when not to speak, where to go and where not to go. The witness efforts would be fruitful because we obey the Spirit of God and have His help.

WHY IS IT IMPORTANT TO MINISTER TO ONE'S OWN CULTURE FIRST?

We are part of a specific culture or ethnicity and there are certain things we hold in common with people in our circle of family, friends and community. We usually have the same language, history, colloquialisms and practices that make us comfortable relating to each other. When we witness to our own people we are witnessing to people much like ourselves. We know the beliefs, life style and practices of our own people. We, like Jesus to the Jews, identify with them and they identify with us. We can speak to them through heritage about cultural practices and prejudices because we have shared them. Others outside this culture would have difficulty communicating with the ethnic group's concerns about daily and personal issues unique to ethnic culture without having some identification problem or cause of offense. The bible was careful to tell us that Jesus knew, cared about and was touched by the infirmities of His people. He was birthed into their culture and was one of them. He, as Moses and the prophets, was one of them and experienced their burdens and limitations. When we become aware of our wicked condition, one of the first things we think is: "Can God save a sinful person like me? Jesus became one of us to be identified with our condition and then He took on Himself all our sins to answer the question of whether we could be saved.

> For we have not an high priest which cannot be touched with the feeling of our infirmities; but was in all points tempted like as we are, yet without sin. Heb 4:15

Jesus took on sin and became as a murderer, adulterer, sexual pervert, thief, liar, and every other sin to identify with us and to atone for our sin. Whatever our sin, and regardless how terrible, He became that and won power over it for us.

Part of my personal testimony is that I was taught how to witness by the Spirit. I was too shy to do much for God but His Spirit would rise up in me to urge me toward His will. A personal example may help to show how God works. As a recently saved and devoted believer, I was zealous about going to church services every time the door opened. In my hurry to go to an evening service, the Holy Spirit stopped me at my apartment in the presence of a neighbor. She had recently moved in and was clearly unsaved by her conduct. The Holy Spirit prompted me to stop and talk to her, which I obeyed. My neighbor made a comment about my practice of hurriedly passing her without taking the time to get to know her. I was so embarrassed and convicted. The lesson learned was that I should not ignore and pass by someone near me, a soul Christ loved, to go to a church across town just to prove how much I loved Him. God was working on me and my environment. As time went on, He led me into witnessing in my neighborhood and city.

Prophet to the People

It is God who has determined through whom His people should receive a message from Him. In the Old Testament He specifically said that He would rise up a speaker, a prophet, from among their own people who would speak to them what He wanted said. When it was time for new direction or instruction, God sent prophets from among their own people to speak to them for Him.

> The LORD thy God will raise up unto thee a Prophet from the midst of thee, of thy brethren, like unto me; unto him ye shall hearken; … I will raise them up a Prophet from among their brethren, like unto thee, and will put my words in his mouth; and he shall speak unto them all that I shall command him. And it shall come to pass, that whosoever will not hearken unto my words which he shall speak in my name, I will require it of him. Deu 18:15-19

> And when this cometh to pass, (lo, it will come,) then shall they know that a prophet hath been among them. Eze 33:33

God was working within the group that was His chosen people because He was their God. He was not directly dealing with the people outside the House of Israel, who were heathen. Rising up a prophet from among them showed God's faithfulness to the promise made to His own people and that He was in the midst of them working for them. It was, first of all, the proof God promised as a sign that He was speaking to the people. God was very emphatic about His people hearing His voice and obeying so He gave them specific instructions about whom to listen to and follow. It was for their protection that He used people they knew.

> If there arise among you a prophet, or a dreamer of dreams, and giveth thee a sign or a wonder, And the sign or the wonder come to pass, whereof he spake unto thee, saying, Let us go after other gods, which thou hast not known, and let us serve them; Thou shalt not hearken unto the words of that prophet, or that dreamer of dreams: for the LORD your God proveth you, to know whether ye love the LORD your God with all your heart and with all your soul. Ye shall walk after the LORD your God, and fear him, and keep his commandments, and obey his voice, and ye shall serve him, and cleave unto him. And that prophet, or that dreamer of dreams, shall be put to death; because he hath spoken to turn you away from the LORD your God, which brought you out of the land of Egypt, and redeemed you out of the house of bondage, to thrust thee out of the way which the LORD thy God commanded thee to walk in. So shalt thou put the evil away from the midst of thee. If thy brother, the son of thy mother, or thy son, or thy daughter, or the wife of thy bosom, or thy friend, which is as thine own soul, entice thee secretly, saying, Let us go and serve other gods, which thou hast not known, thou, nor thy fathers; Namely, of the gods of the people which are round about you, nigh unto thee, or far off from thee, from the one end of the earth even unto the other end of the earth; Thou shalt not consent unto him, nor hearken unto him; neither

> shall thine eye pity him, neither shalt thou spare, neither shalt thou conceal him: But thou shalt surely kill him; thine hand shall be first upon him to put him to death, and afterwards the hand of all the people. And thou shalt stone him with stones, that he die; because he hath sought to thrust thee away from the LORD thy God, which brought thee out of the land of Egypt, from the house of bondage. And all Israel shall hear, and fear, and shall do no more any such wickedness as this is among you. Deu 13:1-11

They would know their prophet because the spokesperson would be one of them. One taken from the midst of them would be known by reputation as honorable or a liar. The supernatural working in the life of one of their own people was a powerful witness. A spokesperson from among them also was proof of God's love and care for their people. Imagine how you would feel if God never spoke to you but always sent a stranger to you to speak for Him. First you would ask yourself: What's wrong with me? Why does He not speak to me? And that does happen when we are in sin. But how about if He went into another country, passing over everyone in your house and town to find a prophet to speak to you? If they were all in the same sinful condition that could happen too like the condition of Sodom. But David's prophet was so near that there was a quick response to David's sin. Today if we obey, God will speak to us by the Holy Spirit.

There are many people and church groups that do not believe God still uses the prophet today but prophets were still being used in the New Testament after the resurrection of Jesus. Jesus spoke of prophets in the past tense and in the future tense.

> Wherefore, behold, I send unto you prophets, and wise men, and scribes: and some of them ye shall kill and crucify; and some of them shall ye scourge in your synagogues, and persecute them from city to city: Mat 23:34

> He that descended is the same also that ascended up far above all heavens, that he might fill all things.) Eph 4:11 And he gave some, apostles; and some, prophets; and some, evangelists; and some, pastors and teachers; For the perfecting of the saints, for the work of the ministry, for the edifying of the body of Christ: Till we all come in the unity of the faith, and of the knowledge of the Son of God, unto a perfect man, unto the measure of the stature of the fulness of Christ: Eph 4:10-13

> And Judas and Silas, being prophets also themselves, exhorted the brethren with many words, and confirmed them. Act 15:32

> And the next day we that were of Paul's company departed, and came unto Caesarea: and we entered into the house of Philip the evangelist, which was one of the seven; and abode with him. And the same man had four daughters, virgins, which did prophesy. And as we tarried there many days, there came down from Judaea a certain prophet, named Agabus. Act 21:8-10

New Testament scripture supports and validates the current use of the gift of prophecy by laypersons in the church and the gift or office of prophets to the church until the body of Christ reaches the position of a perfect man. One has only to look around to see that time has not yet come.

Some churches teach that the pastor is today's prophet but this is not verified by the Eph 4:11 text which lists several offices and positions starting out with apostle, then prophet and later lists the pastor. It is clear that in the Old Testament God preferred to use ministers of Hebrew descent to represent His voice to them and forbade other nations from being their prophets. In cases where there was a need to speak to heathen nations, God sent His prophets to speak for Him. God's prophets, as His spokesperson, can speak to anyone He directs them to but the children of God were directed to hear only their own prophets. They were not allowed to mix with or follow the ways of heathens, who were anybody outside their family. This is validated in the New Testament as well where Jesus taught that His sheep would not hear a stranger. In general practice in life, children are not directed to obey strangers. Believers are taught to know their ministers by their fruit but one cannot judge the fruit of one who is not available for inspection. We know the character traits of those who are close family or of our community and will either trust or distrust them based on what we know. We can also discern the spirit of ministers. God follows His own guidelines though and will use our own people as He stated to be our prophets.

Ensample for the People

The Holy Spirit unites people of every ethnicity into one body where Christ is Lord and the Holy Spirit makes us one family but it takes time to overcome the carnality of our flesh and walk in the spirit. We have to perfect our walk and get along with our own group, let alone dealing with those outside. Though the Grecians were part of the Christian church led by Jewish leaders, there were problems relating to culture where the Grecian widows were neglected in the daily ministration of food (Act 6:1). They continued the Christian fellowship being led by the Holy Spirit after the issue was resolved. And today's church is made up of many nationalities but we are best perfected in our own environment among people that know our ways and can call us on the carpet for questionable behavior before being brought before the world stage.

When we become a Christian, our testimony may be verbal first but it must be witnessed next by our life. If Christ is in us there will be visible changes. Our families will see us witness the ability to adapt to this new way of life. We also witness that they too can overcome the very things that we have to overcome whether they be cultural superstitions, habits, beliefs or long-held traditions. Our new converted life is our first witness to them that they can make the change because we did. That is a pretty powerful witness.

There are many traditions related to the culture of every people of every nation that are based on the traditions of their elders. Even though the truth went out into every nation of people during the days of the early apostles, many nations reverted back to false religions and practices that have evolved into today's false religions. Not only do false cultural practices have to be broken and false religions denounced but people have to be taught against those false practices and learn the new ways of Christ. It takes time, patience and ministry to break the old habits and ways. People do not give up their ways easily. They need to have their questions answered as they try to make the changes necessary in their lives. These questions are best answered by those who know both the old ways and the new so that there is as smooth a transition as possible. The persecution Paul experienced with the old and new ways of the Jews is an example to us of how the enemy will fight the transition of a culture coming to the truth. Everyone involved initially with the new Christian faith was Jewish and yet there was violent resistance to the change. A strong voice was needed to arise and deal with that kind of opposition. God ordained that the apostles and prophets who have knowledge of His ways and possess His power would be able to speak to the people from the heart of God. Even though Christ deals with the heart of man to bring about a change, the head must still receive mental understanding for a balanced life. The early Jewish church dealt with these very kinds of issues.

> And certain men which came down from Judaea taught the brethren, and said, Except ye be circumcised after the manner of Moses, ye cannot be saved. When therefore Paul and Barnabas had no small dissension and disputation with them, they determined that Paul and Barnabas, and certain other of them, should go up to Jerusalem unto the apostles and elders about this question. Act 15:1

> But there rose up certain of the sect of the Pharisees which believed, saying, That it was needful to circumcise them, and to command them to keep the law of Moses. And the apostles and

> elders came together for to consider of this matter. Act 15:5-6

> Wherefore my sentence is, that we trouble not them, which from among the Gentiles are turned to God: But that we write unto them, that they abstain from pollutions of idols, and from fornication, and from things strangled, and from blood. Act 15:19-20

We see in these scriptures that the Christian family had to consider the rituals and traditions to determine if their old tradition should be kept or forsaken. The Jewish leaders understood the history of these rituals that were part of their heritage and relationship with God and that they had no bearing on new believers. The leaders were able to reason with their own people to put away these traditions and walk in the new light. Could you imagine outsiders telling the Jews that their customs were unnecessary? We saw how the Jewish leaders rose up against the Son of God Himself when He talked of changing their traditions. They had been given specific instructions not to listen to those who would try to lead them contrary to the commandments given by Moses. They stoned or killed persons who they considered false teachers for just that kind of reasoning. But those who were led by the heart through the process of obedience to the law first followed John the Baptist into repentance. When they heard Jesus, also one of them, they then understood the rituals were changed through the teaching of Jesus Christ. Even Peter, a Jew, was careful to convince the people that it was God's doing, not his. If we are speaking to family and friends, we share a familiar history, affection for the same traditions; people should have seen evidence of our new life that helps to validate our testimony. The miracle of healings is verified by people who knew the person before the healing. Some changes are a testimony in itself. No one is perfect and some mistakes are made by the best Christians but consistency of a change in the believer's life should evidence God's touch. There will always be naysayers who will never be persuaded because they simply refuse to believe. Jesus pointed this out:

> And he said, Verily I say unto you, No prophet is accepted in his own country. Luk 4:24

Unbelievers may accuse a minister but their witness must never be proven true. Jesus as a True Prophet, though crucified, rose from the grave just as He said He would. Persecution may come but it must not be because the minister is guilty. God will stand up for His faithful witness as He did for the Hebrew boys in the fiery furnace. Even if they were to perish, like many of the patriarchs including John the Baptist, Peter and Christ, they are confirmed and comforted in the crisis and arise victorious and vindicated in heaven. The God who called is able to keep the believer in time of testing or death.

> Let him know, that he which converteth the sinner from the error of his way shall save a soul from death, and shall hide a multitude of sins. Jas 5:20

> And above all things have fervent charity among yourselves: for charity shall cover the multitude of sins. 1Pe 4:8

There will be those that will see the witness of a changed life of someone from their family or culture and be drawn to the Lord through that witness, even watching from afar. Many people observe a believer's life from a distance before ever mentioning to the believer their desire to follow Christ. The believer's steps can be the very steps the new convert will follow to come to a faith in Christ. Christ advised people to follow Him but the witness of Christ should be in the church leader as well. Paul advised people to follow him as he followed Christ. People desire to see Christ in us before they set out to follow our example to reach Christ. It is, of course, easier to follow a path that we can see and understand than one that must be translated or converted to our cultural understanding. Christ emphasized the importance of His works and miracles as visible evidence that backed up His claim of communion with God. He taught us about using the establishment of two or three witnesses for validation of truth (Mat 18:16). He taught of the importance of fruit bearing witness of our Christian life and that we show forth works that validate our testimony. Christ told the people that if they did not believe His words then believe Him for the works He performed. So the life we live before people and the evidence they see does validate our testimony that we know God. To witness a life and follow implies a position of closeness where one is able to discern the path of the believer.

HOW NON-ETHNIC MINISTERS CAN PRESENT DIFFICULTY FOR ETHNIC CONGREGATION?

We have already shown that God and Christ directed people to hear their own people first and that these ministers later traveled to other nations as well. The Old Testament scripture promises that God will use prophets or leaders from among us that we know. In the New Testament instructions of Ephesians Chapter Four and also in others books on church order, we are told the offices of a local church that we submit to. These scripture references depict the order of a house or family, where there is a head authority in charge. Apostle Paul both established and exercised lead authority over the churches he established. He denounced outsiders and warned the people of following false leaders. He was a Jewish leader over gentile churches but they also had other local leadership of elders, most likely of their own people.

We have discussed some examples where there are difficulties when non-ethnic ministers try to minister to people of other ethnicities. Gentile believers were being required by the Jews to adhere to Jewish rites such as circumcision. The people of Lystra (Acts 14) wanted to make gods out of Paul and Barnabus after a man was healed and later stoned them. There is no personal identification with a minister having a different culture than the people. They cannot be examples of how to overcome the areas of sin and practices of another culture that they have never experienced. Many people have sins based on heritage, cultural practices and familial habits that are rooted in societal practices and celebrations that are inherited through prior generations. People are reluctant to accept the testimony of people who have never gone through what they are going through and they are quick to say "you just don't understand" because you never experienced it. Paul and other apostles witnessed Christ but left the churches in the hand of local leaders and elders who directly led the new converts. We want people to believe our testimony to them but a testimony is the story of how we overcame obstacles or sins to obtain our present victory. Our life is to be a type of roadmap to them of how they too can overcome like we did. But people of a different culture may not be a visible roadmap of how to overcome problems they have never encountered. When one is in the trenches, he does not want just to hear a sermon that all things are possible with God; what he wants are specific and relevant steps to take, rather than theology.

Believing Jews could testify from the heart about the problems they encountered trying to obey the Law of Moses. The Law was only given to the Israelites so they were the best witnesses to the Jews of how to overcome the Law's grip and believe by faith. Paul, as a past Pharisee, was able to witness how he overcame loyalty to that teaching and achieved faith in Christ. Peter was able to witness to other Jews how he had to overcome adherence to Jewish laws and prejudice against the gentiles because he experienced those problems. People tend to believe that if a person just like them can overcome, then so can they. This identification with the sinner can make the witnessing more effective and it was God's idea when He chose to send a Jewish Son to speak to the Jews and a human body, even a man, to witness to men who led Jewish homes.

Even though anyone can witness for Christ, they cannot be the best witness of overcoming obstacles they never encountered. White people, for instant, cannot tell black people how to overcome a slave mentality or the racial prejudice from white people because they were never subjected to these social and mental obstacles that blacks have experienced. White people can teach black people to believe by faith but blacks will still have the challenges of overcoming prejudiced attitudes toward their physical characteristics. Mental, social and financial hindrances are part of everyday life of the typical African American. It is difficult to receive help in these areas from ministers of other ethnicities who have never encountered these problems. They may suggest the answer to a financial problem is to go get a loan, where a black person may already know that getting the loan is a problem all by itself. These ministers may give their best instructions but still leave something missing in the witness. One can tell the minister of the complexities but he cannot relate to the different cultural issues. The witness may not ring true to the believer because the speaker has no identification or depth of understanding of the problem. It also fails the test of a true prophet: a spokesperson from among you as a witness. There are other abnormalities unique to the black community based on heritage or social ails that cannot be ministered to by those who cannot identify with or understand those ailments. Jesus is a sufficient comforter and minister because He was touched with all our infirmities and knows intimately our sufferings. This knowledge and identification with our pain was so important that God put on a flesh body, became a human living in our neighborhood and subjected Himself to our experiences.

Christ came so that we could be made whole again from our broken lives. Every broken area in our life must be touched by the finger of God. Someone must help us to know what is broken so that we can seek healing. When we listen to the testimony of one like us who has overcome our type of problem, it helps us believe that we can overcome also. When we hear testimonies from others like us, we receive help in areas we did not know were broken. Christ became one of us to identify with us and bring healing to every broken part of our lives. He wants us to have complete healing and wholeness in every area. In our church circles, the Holy Spirit will provide witness, instructions and healing for every broken area. The body will minister healing to itself. Those that have overcome some abnormality will witness, minister and teach others how they can overcome as well. The minister's identification with others becomes an important factor in convincing new believers of the possibility of their success as well. Children imitate their adult parents and baby Christians imitate their spiritual leaders. They see what they can become. Like Thomas, those that are carnal-minded need a witness to be persuaded of spiritual truths. They watch the life and follow the leader's testimony and likeness until they can see Christ for themselves. Peter witnessed Jesus up close and followed His steps all the way to the cross and a throne reserved for him in heaven. Paul taught that he would have us prosper and receive wholeness in the spirit, soul and body. Failing to receive some area of healing whether spiritual, mental or physical leaves one with an unbalanced life. They may gain faith and knowledge without an actual healing in the hindered area. Christ came to bring total healing to every area of our life so that our joy would be complete. Following His instructions leads us to that balanced, joyful and whole life in spirit, soul and body. The goal for every person is total restoration to the pre-curse fellowship.

> Brethren, be followers together of me, and mark them which walk so as ye have us for an ensample. Php 3:17

> Those things, which ye have both learned, and received, and heard, and seen in me, do: and the God of peace shall be with you. Php 4:9

The purpose of Christ was to win families and communities to the ways of God that would restore peaceful fellowship in our lives with family, society and God. Interactions and identification with successful leaders in our own people can help us work out inner turmoil pertaining to our ethnicity and heal us as a people. Black boys in the black community need to see strong black leaders in all areas to imagine they can also reach these positions. This is not realized by placing one in another cultural environment where they are stripped of their own cultural identity and forced to learn acceptance and new practices in another society. In such a situation the person may learn to hide or avoid certain tenacities or sins that may not be acceptable or tolerated in the new environment. He may feel a need to be artificial or perform to fit in with people of other ethnic backgrounds or cultures. This denial of one's true self does not bring the joy and fulfillment in one's soul that only truth can provide.

For purposes of identification, missionaries often teach ethnic people how to minister to their own people with whose culture they identify. Indian people know the cultural practices of Indian people and they can tell their own people how to overcome some beliefs and practices of the Indian culture. Their environment is improved through their witness and conversion of their family and friends. They remain in their own community with their ethnic culture as it progresses rather than their being disenfranchised from family and friends to learn Christ. They are saved and made whole in their environment. When Christ comes into this ethnic environment, He begins to bring correction and balance that improves all aspects the environment. He knows what to keep and what needs to be thrown out. He does not stripe the people of their culture or history but instead perfects it. This is the best way to improve ethnic communities where there are ethnic related issues. There will be questions from new converts that only people of your own culture can address effectively. People who had strange religious practices will want answers about it that one who has shared those experiences can answer without causing offense. When such a one is saved and returns to his own environment, it is improved by Christ's presence.

There is a custom of people in America to adopt babies from overseas nations like China, Japan or Russia. Many of these lives are made better by coming into America but they are, nevertheless, removed from their own cultures and become Americanized. That transition may or may not work out for them but surely at some point they will want to know about and perhaps visit their past culture. There is an instinct in people that causes them to want to know who they are, where they came from and who are their people. We see this trait often in children who are adopted within American borders. Their self-identity and worth has to be validated by their family. They are only one part of a whole entity and they are reinforced when they see, understand and are accepted in that group. With the best possible adopted parents, many still want to know their birth parents and family. We are healed in part until we becomed healed in whole but we all seek to be whole.

There are problems which occur within cultures and nations that must be dealt with by people of those classes of people. The Greek widows had spokesperson who spoke up for them about being mistreated as a class and it was dealt with by the church. Their problems were not realized by the Israelites until the Greek people addressed it as a problem in their Greek community. The Israelites were not aware or experiencing this problem so it had to be addressed by a Greek spokesperson. This biblical example is there for our example. It shows that in the Christian church among believers, there are still issues that must be addressed pertaining to the culture or ethnicity of the people and how much more in the unsaved world. Because there are some ministers that do not have the shared problems of their congregation, they, therefore, cannot identify or minister to many of the issues for which their members must contend and these people may not become truly whole, missing their full destiny.

There may be some who read this information and think that it is an effort to bring separation or prejudice into the church fellowship. However, in America one would have to admit that Sunday is already considered the most segregated hour. Many problems already exist and are in need of solution. Ignoring them has not caused them to go away. Churches in every racial group are set up by and for people of their racial background and it is the best place to deal with cultural issues that find no place in the political discussion. Many ethnic problems exist because of lack of resources and rights for people to become whole in our society. Problems break out because people are seeking their wholeness in a broken society. Sometimes in their ignorance or desperation, they seek the wrong thing or way to accomplish their wholeness. Efforts to heal our community come and go every four years as political leaders are voted in and out. Political leaders try to make decisions in the lives of people they do not know, understand and sometimes do not care about. Sometimes boiling pots boil over.

There comes a time when we have to deal with the root of our problems. Those that understand and care are the best intercessors for those problems. If one continues to read, it will be made plain that this author supports every nationality and the unity of the brethren of all cultures and ethnicities into the church and body of Christ. However, just as the problem with the Greek widows had to be brought to the surface and dealt with, it is also true of our racial problems in America. Some sicknesses in the body require a specialist and some members of the body require special healing from specific ministers. To ignore this need is to allow some members to die needlessly from ailments that could have received healing. Christ cares about every one of our abnormalities. Every limb must be healed for the body to be whole. He wants to bring healing for our total deliverance, joy and peace. The Holy Spirit is intent on finding a way to minister to every need. He does not leave anyone or group to carry the burden or hurt alone without reaching out through His love to care for them. We should observe that in the New Testament examples where we see salvation coming to whole families and community, the family unity was preserved and their salvation impacted their environment (Lk 8:39-40).

Once the gospel is taught and Jesus is made Lord of the congregation, there are still many social practices and obstacles that must be overcome that the ministers of other cultures cannot begin to address without appearing superior or offensive. When they say the word "we", immediately there is the question of identification. To whom are they referring: people of their race, gender, religious calling, or faith. We heal in part before we become whole. The Christian community must deal with social issues like that shown in the story of the Greek widows who were being neglected or the superstition and witchcraft shown in Acts 19. The Christian community must deal with and overcome prejudiced attitudes, obstacles in the community by addressing the real issues and bringing permanent solution rather than just allowing the dominant race to overpower the weak and defenseless to have their own way in a spirit of superiority. Elders or mature leaders of ethnic communities must deal with these types of issues. Every person was made in the image of God and has worth and value. The plan of God is to redeem every limb and person of the body without exception. God works through humankind and we are His instruments to do His work in the earth. We have to learn more perfectly how He wants to work in our churches and environment to bring wholeness. He says every soul belongs to Him and He warns that the hurt of the least of His children is hurt to Him. It cannot be over looked. He especially comforts the downtrodden.

EVERY NATION MUST BE RECONCILED BACK TO GOD

Issues in Black and White

Black and white people are at opposite ends of the color spectrum and every other ethnicity are racial mixtures from interracial unions that fall between the two. If we could solve the racial issues between these two people, we have a strong possibility of solving all the others. It is important to note though that this is primarily an American issue. In many other countries around the world, color or race is not a major issue because their population is mostly bi-racial and made up of ethnic communities. Europe had already received correction on slavery issues through evangelism before the pioneers crossed the seas and formed America. The really sad fact and as stated at the beginning of this discussion, all races come out of the African continent and the black race. Some whites have discovered their roots and are now in denial and are fighting to destroy that truth and the blacks that represent it.

African Americans are descendants of slaves from the continent of Africa who were brought to America unwillingly in chains to serve white people. Blacks built the foundation of the nation by their free labor. These African descendants are people who are the descendants of the African intellectuals whose knowledge and wisdom was stolen from Africa and taken to Greece, Rome and subsequently used as the foundational knowledge of the Western world. Much of the foundational knowledge of America from architect, medicine, math and science comes from African intellect. American history books omit this important piece of information. The conquering and exploited power exercised by the European nations that explored and consumed the wealth of other nations, is still being practiced in America against descendants of their former slaves. The imperialist spirit of past European nations that conquered nations and people to promote themselves still shows up in their European descendants. The civility of the democratic process in America had until recently kept people from public displays of oppressive actions but America is seeing a new day where darkness has come out in the open to challenge past democratic restraints. The sentiment and process was always there but it was worked in hidden ways through rules and policies by white citizens and government officials. Their determination to keep black people oppressed and subdued is exercised through many known and unknown programs but it is an undercurrent in the nation of America that is not publicly acknowledged. Laws and practices are established that target the black community to keep them as a subclass of the majority white society. Stricter penalties for crime and illegal arrests are some of the injustices brought against blacks. Civil protests against injustices bring more injustice from white America. Black people in America are facing racism and political deafness on the one end of the spectrum in a supposedly Christian nation while participating in a gospel often led by white ministers who claim God loves blacks while they support and promote politicians on the other end who refuse black equality and resources in the nation. Christianity stands for grace and truth which Jesus came to bring to all the earth. White leaders that profess Christ are also promoting lies, racist policies and concealing the truth from the black population, who support their ministries with their dollars. America is finding true the words of American poet, Emma Lazarus: "Until we are all free, we are none of us free."

A recent article in Christianity Today magazine made clear where American society and Christian church stand today. The June 2017 article is entitled: "Repenting of Superiority" where a Ugandan Anglican Bishop, David Zac Niringiye, educated in an American college and living in Africa, enlightened an American charitable outreach for Africa. Here is an excerpt:

> "A young American white man asked me, 'Bishop Zac, how can we help you?'" recounted theologian, pastor, and HIV/AIDS activist David Zac Niringiye, in a talk addressing the Christianity Today staff this spring. "I thanked him for that question and I said, 'That's precisely the issue. Who told you I need your help?'" Bishop Zac has no qualms about challenging people's assumptions—especially with regards to the West's beliefs about Africa. "Brother, we don't need your help," he said, as he

> continued the story. "Why? Because there is another false narrative which is the narrative of superiority. Let me be bold: white America, you have a challenge because you have a narrative of superiority." White American Christians were not the only ones susceptible to narratives, he suggested."[There's] a myth that created a certain narrative about what it means to be African. An African feels inferior to a white man. That is a tragedy," he said. "...What Africans must do is repent of this view of inferiority. We must take responsibility for our narratives." According to Bishop Zac, the continent's difficulties don't stem from the usual suspects, like poverty or HIV/AIDS. "It's a confidence crisis," he said. "Many years of colonial oppression created a situation in which Africans started to believe they were inferior."(3)

Christ taught that Christians were brethren and equal partners in the bounty of the land and blessings of the kingdom. American white Christian ministries are failing to promote this message for education and improvement of the American population. Jesus rightly called the religious leaders of the Temple hypocrites. How much more so are religious leaders who behave in such prejudiced ways and still profess to serve Christ? White Christian slave masters taught African slaves they were cursed and less than human. They used the bible and fear of God to teach blacks submission and humility to all white people. They have never, as a people or nation, confessed this sin. The truly Christian white majority in America could have long ago dealt with the racial inequalities in America. When they dare speak about the problems because some new issue has arisen, they fail to follow through with corresponding action. Not only are white churches not prepared to deal with many racial issues but they have not shown proper Christian concern for them. When true salvation comes to your house, you are more inclined to love and help your neighbor no matter what color they are. Salvation is an internal working of spirit and soul that affects outward behavior. If God has greatly blessed you, there should be genuine thankfulness in a desire to help heal others. History records many prominent Christians though who were slave masters so there was evidently something missing in their Christian experience that they did not deal with.

Promotion of the Christian religion and its marketing are a major economic force in America. There is no end to the modern technology used by American Christians and the media outlets are state of the art. Christian preaching is non-stop on 24-hour broadcasts and no manner of resource is denied or withheld from them. Yet the word of God has already diagnosed this problem and this time:

> This know also, that in the last days perilous times shall come. For men shall be lovers of their own selves, covetous, boasters, proud, blasphemers, disobedient to parents, unthankful, unholy, Without natural affection, trucebreakers, false accusers, incontinent, fierce, despisers of those that are good, Traitors, heady, highminded, lovers of pleasures more than lovers of God; Having a form of godliness, but denying the power thereof: from such turn away. For of this sort are they which creep into houses, and lead captive silly women laden with sins, led away with divers lusts, Ever learning, and never able to come to the knowledge of the truth. 2 Tim 3:1-7

Those of the white race have multiplied their wealth and gone around the world preaching to every nation with the intent of fulfilling:

> Mat 24:14 And this gospel of the kingdom shall be preached in all the world for a witness unto all nations; and then shall the end come.

White Christians have installed satellites that reach around the world, use 24-hour preaching fundraisers and have translated the bible into nearly every language; and yet the world and particularly America seems to be headed back into the dark ages. As I write this on August 14, 2017, America witnessed on yesterday white nationalists, neo-Nazis and the KKK rallying at University of Virginia, in Charlottesville, Virginia, to support white supremacy and to protest the removal of the memorial statute for the general who fought to preserve slavery and surrendered his army during the

American Civil War, Confederate General Robert E. Lee. The rally was met with mostly white anti-fascist protesters, one of whom was intentionally run down and killed by a car driven by a member of the nationalist group. The situation was made all the more appalling and alarming when the new President, Donald Trump, whose campaign was endorsed by the KKK leader and other racist groups, failed to give an immediate response of condemnation; and when he did speak, failed to denounce and rebuke the radical forces of the nationalists who promoted violence. There were outcries from nearly every corner about the President's failure to uphold morality and the democratic process. Though many may have been appalled at their president, the truth is that he ran on the support of and was elected by the very groups that embarrassed the nation with a racist Sunday demonstration watched by the world.

The nation may have been appalled at the actions of the President but the hidden sentiment of a majority of white people in the nation was expressed through those representatives. Christian evangelical churches, republicans, KKK, Neo-Nazis and other racists combined their power to elect a racist as president. Members of the President's cabinet were hand-picked specifically to advance racist programs that would turn the clock backward on racial equity. That statement is not an opinion because the media has done daily reports investigating and validating these intents before the American people. The first six months of this American presidency has proven and revealed the intent to target for deletion social programs and civil rights bills that support blacks, other minorities and the poor. Even die-hard republican congressional leaders had to come out and speak against the president's openly prejudiced remarks that denied the blame of the nationalists. They were not necessarily against his efforts but it had never been done so openly in public eyes and with such boldness and reckless disregard for diplomacy.

In America today every hidden sin has come forward and demanded it share of the light. These are sins that have been dominant in America for generations although previously kept in the dark. In America's latter days, her sins have found her out. America has to now admit its dark underbelly because it is no longer hidden. Now that the ugliest parts of America have been exposed to the world, it is time for America to deal with its sins that has never been done before. Like the issue of guns in the mass murder of children in schools and other victims, America does not want to do anything that will hurt the rights of whites or affect their economic empowerment. People ask at times of atrocities in their midst, where is God? God is where He has always been; in heaven watching mankind in obedience and disobedience. He still has all power but He has assigned mankind as His priests and stewards over the land. Should He now come down and take it back? He will in time, but not just yet.

God required His ministers to go to their own nation and preach Jesus before trying to tackle the problems of the world. Their own culture was to be their testing and proving ground before tackling world issues. They were literally supposed to clean their own house before trying to clean ethnic groups and the earth of sin. The radical groups that have come forth show a failure in the white Christian evangelistic efforts. These recurring outbreaks show a need of evangelism in the white community. This problem had not been dealt with by the white Christian evangelistic teams before reaching out to the rest of the world to save the lost in other nations. We have seen the white leadership cut down and subdue black militants of the past decades who rallied for blacks until they are barely heard of anymore. When any radical or prominent black groups arise today to speak up for equality in the black population, the white leaders immediately respond to denounce and subdue its voice and any possible impact in the black community. Their control of politics, media, religious outlets and now the Presidency gives them the upper hand against black activism. The black population has been contained down through the years by many forces and methods but the white community does not seem to have the same outrage or desire to subdue its own radical groups. This was their outcry to the American Muslims who they believed should have stood up and protested against Muslim terrorism and ISIS. Yet the white elites nor its evangelists will stand up and do it. Hypocrisy is showing up in these Christian leaders

Christian ministries are going all over the world trying to preach a message that is not even working in their own back yard. Racist ministries, organizations, politicians, employers and the local citizens are rising up with great racial hatred, Christian assaults and slurs while the white majority Christian church and community continues to preach the same gospel messages to the same people with little effect on these communities. The little rag tag ministries of Peter, James and Paul turned the world upside down with little or nothing in worldly goods while the extravagance of the modern white church seems ineffective in leading the world to the true love of God. Multi-million dollar administrative buildings, staff and jet planes have not accomplished what Peter, James and Paul accomplished without them.

While the white Christian ministries in America are reaching out to the black community with ministry and receiving their financial support, they are silent at racial outbursts, hide their claim to racial superiority and refuse the sharing of economic resources and authority among the descendants of those whom their ancestors enslaved and exploited for centuries and whom they still oppose by racist policies, while professing Christian faith. Even though it has been proven through scientific and archeological communities of America that bible history is that of a black population, human life started on the continent of Africa, and that the wisdom of the western world was stolen from African scholars, white Americans and Christian ministries refuse to bring this knowledge forward in their churches and the community, for healing of the races, to reconcile history, bring financial empowerment for their former slave population or contain the radical anti-ethnic forces promoting white supremacy in hope of an all-white nation. In their silence, they win regardless because they are in the majority and protect their class. Their failure to correct their own radical groups, reconcile past racial hatred and withdraw their superiority posture reveals an unrepentant state that cannot be Christian. Their concern would more properly be directed to learn what is missing in their salvation experience that would allow them to sit in silence at the atrocities in the nation and their lack of love for their Christian "brethren". They cannot bring unity among the races and heal the nation until they first heal themselves. This puts the black population in such ministries at a disadvantage because their minister does not acknowledge this truth and cannot lead them into total restoration. Jesus taught that the truth would make us free but these believers are being denied the truth of their natural and spiritual rights. Though they may teach and share with their congregation biblical principles, something will, nevertheless, be missing because of their failure to deal with issues of the soul or bring forth truth. The Christian gospel does not automatically resolve social issues. Christianity must be practiced in truth to change the world. Humans are required to carry the light of Jesus into the dark place. Jesus came to bring us truth that would subdue the devil's influences and make us free.

> And ye shall know the truth, and the truth shall make you free. Joh 8:32

Sinners come into the church to hear the truth that will set them free from the bondage they are under through a life of service to the devil. If the church does not tell the whole truth that sets one free then it is making Jesus into a lie. God told the prophet to eat the whole loath and then speak that which he has heard in the ear to the people. Truth about one's racial heritage that has been hidden and a history of racial servitude to a dominant race is a pretty strong reason for ethnic people having ministers of their own cultural background. We notice in the book of Philemon that Paul brought spiritual deliverance and salvation to Onesimus, a slave, and then wrote a letter to his believing owner to now consider the slave in his true worth and the slave master's own indebtedness to Paul. Paul led the slave master to consider the grace of Jesus Christ and recommended him to his own conscience.

Another conflict may develop when Christians who are black in America submit to white Christian ministers where the minster supports a political party with racist candidates or that is backed by anti-black groups. Those blacks in these churches may have difficulty deciding between their social well-being as blacks and their Christian beliefs. God is not the author of confusion and does not require Christians to dissolve or repute their cultural connections. He both recognizes and watches over the care of all people and nations. The Greek widows were still identifiable as Greek but had to speak up and demand proper treatment from their Christian brothers.

In a larger society like America, some problems are bigger than one's individual church and must be dealt with on a national scale. Black Christian churches are best able to make a demand on the white Christian churches and call it into Christian love and equality. This demand would perhaps be made except that the black church has been deceived by the prosperity gospel promoted primarily by white churches. Their lack of empowerment in the white world has caused some to seek money at the expense of their own people's spiritual wellbeing. Some ministers have been silent because of fear of retribution, government regulations, white influence or sin. This surely cannot be done by a white minister, who does not understand the issue or the need for change. Neither blacks nor whites can overcome the devil's lies by operating in timidity. The church of Jesus Christ must be strong in the midst of these troubling times. America white Christians have failed to deal with racial prejudice in the church and society for too long. Their majority rule and Christian profession puts them under the greater responsibility to correct these problems. "To whom much is given shall much be required (Lk 12:48)." The nation cannot continue to survive these reoccurring problems that have deepened, rather than improve. How can I say that so emphatically? I can say it because Jesus already prophesied it:

> And Jesus knew their thoughts, and said unto them, Every kingdom divided against itself is brought to desolation; and every city or house divided against itself shall not stand: Mat12:25

History debates the cause for the fall of the powerful Greek and Roman empires but internal turmoil from within certainly were contributing factors. America has too many powerful examples in history to miss this lesson that elementary children study.

Christianity as Unifier

Peter tried to deal with the issue of Jewish traditions imposed upon the gentiles but was found in hypocritical conflict even after the direct intervention and teaching from Christ. Peter was very absorbed in the Jewish traditions and had difficulty relinquishing them. We are seeing that the Christian faith in America has not brought about the relinquishing of ungodly controlling power and privileges by white Christians in America. They like Peter find it difficult to relinquish traditions and adapt to the requirement of inclusion for all new citizens in the Kingdom of God. Astute Christian ministers with the highest caliber of resources and Christian knowledge deny the very gospel of inclusion for every believer as Christ taught.

Black Christians and other ethnic believers are thought of as second class or an under-class by whites, contrary to the teachings of Christ. The wealth, liberty, knowledge and confession of Christ require them to rectify this sin. Christ spoke to the early church that there were many others to be brought into the fold and that there would be one shepherd and one fold but the majority of white Americans have not shown the willingness to accept Christian doctrine above racial preferences. Christian faith in a predominantly Christian nation would require Christians to denounce territorial control and adapt to a unified church with equality among the citizens and brethren.

Some "elite" Christians are like the ancient Gnostics consumed with visions while they talk of revival and repentance without actually repenting of well-known sin. Their visions and revelations of God fail to reveal their own sins or the way to racial healing. Their Jesus does not talk to them about how to solve America's dilemma. The first Christian apostles addressed issues that divided the Christian body and brought resolution but today's elite white Christians will not move the church to a healing place for jeopardy of losing their standing in the body or their wealthy positions. To the contrary our noted Christian American ministries are preaching a prosperity gospel that promotes piling up wealth for themselves and teaching a false gospel to the poor that causes them to send their resources to these wealthy preachers. Is this the same gospel Paul preached? The truth of the gospel is being withheld from them while they are being exploited by a lie spun in hell. Peter and Paul's gospel taught love of neighbor and brought ethnic groups together in Christian unity. First century Christians were warned of accepting another gospel or another Jesus (2Co 11:4). Christ is Lord over all people; His goodness is toward all people. He does not condone this unrighteousness nor is He silent about it in scripture.

> God that made the world and all things therein, seeing that he is Lord of heaven and earth, dwelleth not in temples made with hands; Neither is worshipped with men's hands, as though he needed any thing, seeing he giveth to all life, and breath, and all things; And hath made of one blood all nations of men for to dwell on all the face of the earth, and hath determined the times before appointed, and the bounds of their habitation… Act 17:24-26

> For there are many unruly and vain talkers and deceivers, specially they of the circumcision: Whose mouths must be stopped, who subvert whole houses, teaching things which they ought not, for filthy lucre's sake. Tit 1:10-11

> I marvel that ye are so soon removed from him that called you into the grace of Christ unto another gospel: Which is not another; but there be some that trouble you, and would pervert the gospel of Christ. But though we, or an angel from heaven, preach any other gospel unto you than that which we have preached unto you, let him be accursed. Gal 1:6-8

Christians and especially spirit filled Christians used to be ridiculed and talked about because other denominations like Baptists, Methodists or Presbyterians were the elites of church society. Holy people and tongue talkers were frowned on and ridiculed. That table has long ago turned and spirit-filled people and tongue-talkers are in most denominations as the elite churches of America that fill stadiums, theaters and mega centers. Jesus' name had come to the forefront and need not be whispered anymore. Multi-millions dollars are spent with Christian services, broadcasts, books, videos and other paraphernalia. If there was ever a time for Christians to boldly stand and declare the power of Jesus, it is today. Christianity has won over many former competing religions and even they now acknowledge the name of Jesus. Some may denounce His deity but still make sure they acknowledge that they too believe in Jesus. There is a time when things come to maturity and we can see its fruit and of what source it is. So is the fruit of white Christianity of God or of man? Is their Jesus the one of the scriptures that is being preached or is it another Jesus? Is it the same Jesus who ran the merchandisers out of the temple because of their love of money over a relationship with God? If it is not God's fruit then it calls for repentance. This is the turning point, where a height has been reached, whether right or wrong, and we can either correct errors and move forward toward the rapture or return back to the darkness. Repenting of error and moving forward is the best path to take. There is no sin Jesus will not forgive, excluding blasphemy against the Holy Spirit. His arms are still open to the repentant soul but there must be true repentance and a real turning from sin.

WHY NON-ETHNIC MINISTERS CAN BE A DETRIMENT TO ETHNIC CHURCH?

There is a tenancy for people of some ethnic backgrounds to put down their own ethnic group because of the group's lack of knowledge and resources while believing that people from the more dominate cultures are more informed, spiritual or intellectual than their own people. It is unhealthy to despise one's own people because of lack or disadvantage. These people may develop an unhealthy need to be accepted or validated by the dominant group. This can put ethnic people at a disadvantage if they regard these ministers, their ministries or people as something more sacred or give them a place reserved for God alone. Believers may be willing to make harmful compromises to remain in such a church or follow its leader. Bishop Zac was quoted earlier in the Christianity Today article as saying: "Many years of colonial oppression created a situation in which Africans started to believe they were inferior."(3) God is redeeming every people and restoring us to wholeness. Jesus told believers to follow Him and He supplants our weak state with His perfection.

In recent elections for president of the United States, people and groups of all types were splintered because ethnic and moral decisions had to be made. Minorities had to decide between what was best for their ethnic group concerning social rights and the best Christian decision because of the atrocity of the abortion issue. The candidate favoring minorities did not support the Christian moral point of view and the candidate that supported the moral viewpoint had no concern for ethnic people. These kinds of decisions can be very difficult to maneuver and the ethnic community must decide what is best for it. A Christian leader of the non-ethnic majority race may well be inclined to advise the moral decision to the disregard of the ethnic believer's concern about his racial disadvantage in society. Neither choice may be suitable to the advantage of the ethnic believer where ethnic views are not counted valuable to the candidate. This type of conflict divides the power of blacks and their ability to advocate for better rights in America.

America was formed from European immigrants whose ancestors were part of once strong nations that defined their identities. Europe was ruled at various times by conquerors and imperialist-minded people, who were constantly warring to survive, enrich and empower themselves. Those words are awkward in American culture because America is made up of people from many nations who have decided to live under a democracy where all people are provided for under a united umbrella and the federal government.

Everybody comes from somewhere and everybody has a history. Our genes and nature are patterned after our ancestry. A background from imperialist nations produces people influenced by their genetics to dominate and rule as superiors. Those characteristics may be subdued in democracy but the spiritual and mental tendencies are still there. For example: Regardless of how long African descendants have been in America, we are still spirited people who love to sing and dance much like our ancestors. Our singing and dancing are different now but we are still a singing and dancing people, even in our church worship. That is our nature. Imperialists, on the other hand, love to conquer and rule others and that is in their nature. Despite democracy there is a nature of conquering and ruling that comes out in the superiority attitude of the white majority in America even while pursuing a relationship with God. They are descended from a domineering or conquering people and the trait seem to be in their DNA. Regardless of efforts for black people to obtain equal rights in America, the white government and its citizens find ways to block those efforts. That is the characteristic of a spirit of superiority or imperialists. When the so called domiciled whites seem to relax in democracy, the radical whites arise to demand that the white race rule in supremacy. It is a spirit that refuses to compromise.

There was an article in Christianity Today that seems to illustrate this point. A black minister named John Perkins was born in Mississippi and wrote about his experience with race issues in a March 2017 article entitled, "John Perkins: I Wish I Had Done More to Help Poor White People." Here are some excerpts:

> "In Hebron, Mississippi, I grew up around poor whites who felt they were better than blacks and expected us to move out of their way when they were walking down the street. They experienced all of the advantages of being white. They were oppressors, and common knowledge through the years was that in rural areas, poor whites sought to become sheriffs, cops, or guards in order to have some power over society. So we did not have a great relationship with them. At the time, I didn't realize these whites had also been damaged and that oppressing blacks gave them a sense of worth—a twisted sense of value, no doubt, but in their eyes, value nonetheless.
>
> The wealthy whites also used the poor whites as tools of oppression, making them overseers or guards or sheriffs charged

with taking care of the dirty work to keep black people in their place so they didn't have to. In reality, though, this just fueled the resentment between black and poor whites."(4)

Ultimately, the church knows that the fight is one of principalities against principalities, spirits and spiritual warfare. Because these problems are primarily spiritual at the root, it is the responsibility of spiritually mature churches to respond to the urgent need in the community. These spiritual problems are fought in the natural over skin color and possessions. The same types of fights go on in homes, jobs and communities as people seek to have authority over others for their personal advantage. A fairer economic system that makes provision for all its citizen to have jobs or income that meet their basic need with chances of upward mobility could reduce the amount of crime and violence in our community that are often motivated by the poor seeking their portion of provision. Inevitably some people will always seek more than their just portion through taking from others and laws are in place for just punishment. Whatever the fight, we must defend our right to life and liberty in the natural and in the spirit.

When confronted with a multi-ethnic group and cultural difficulties in the early church, a meeting of leaders was called and the Holy Spirit consulted. The cultural beliefs and differences had to be dealt with in a manner that kept peace in the body. A decision was made that considered the needs of both groups and satisfied their moral conscience. They read the word of God which is God's mind on every problem and the church leaders submitted to the wise council of the Holy Spirit. The religious and spirit-filled leaders were able to bring minds, spirits and bodies into obedience through sound doctrine and reasoning. Leaders of another culture may not understand or be concerned about these struggles within an ethnic group.

In excerpts from another article from Christianity Today, we have a view of the opinion of white Christian evangelicals about race. The 2016 article is entitled: "Evangelicals and Race – A New Chapter" by Mark Galli.

> "Evangelicals are sensitive to what we call "God moments"—when circumstances fall together in a way that suggests God is at work in our lives in a fresh way.
>
> Mainstream white evangelicals have experienced collective "God moments." In the 1970s, few churches concerned themselves with the relief of world hunger…we quickly saw the great evil that abortion is. These were God moments—times when our Lord graciously gave us moral clarity about an issue he was calling us to engage.
>
> We are currently experiencing a new "God moment," when God is shining his burning light on how our nation and churches are fractured by racial division and injustice. In the past two years, we've seen image after image of injustice perpetrated against black Americans. We've studied the statistics. And most important, we've heard the anguished cry of a suffering community that is understandably hurting, angry, and demanding progress.
>
> Moderate white evangelicals, who make up the bulk of our movement, see more clearly than ever how racism is embedded in many aspects of our society, from business to law enforcement to education to church life. we have been slow to hear what the black church has been telling us for a while. And in all that, we hear God calling his church to seek justice and reconciliation in concrete ways."(5)

Some of those words are encouraging except that the article identifies their slowness to respond to these troubles and the amount of time they dedicate to racial issues. The urgency of these problems cannot wait on the convenience of white evangelicals. These statements given in mid-2016 are followed by the mid-2017 outburst of racial upheaval.

> "To be evangelical now means to be no longer deaf to these cries or to God's call. In 2012, only 13 percent of white evangelicals said they thought about race daily. (41% black evangelicals did so). Today, we're thinking about race more than daily—due

> partly to the news cycle, and partly to our rediscovering biblical teaching."(5)

The next excerpts of a 2016 article entitled, 'The Church at Its Racial Turning Point", also from Christianity Today reveals the conflict within Christian evangelicals.

> In this moment, American churches face the challenge and opportunity of addressing what some consider America's "original sin." A 2012 survey found that most evangelicals believe "one of the most effective ways to improve race relations is to stop talking about race." More and more Christians realize that in order to do something, we cannot avoid these discussions or remain silent as society around us grapples with such an embedded issue.
>
> The violence against police suggests that society stands on the brink of a chaotic response as a result or racial turmoil unmatched since the 1965 Watts Riots, which resurfaced in the 1992 Rodney King riots. The current crisis highlights the disconnect between black and white perspectives on race relations and exposes a growing impatience in minority communities with persistent and systemic forms of racism. The potential for positive change seems more distant now than any time in recent memory.
>
> Evangelicals enthusiastically embrace the cause of the unborn. This fervor stems from believe in the sanctity of life. This same concern lies at the heart of #BlackLivesMatter. But they often fail to notice how black and brown youth are treated as less than human, how they face the inequalities in education, employment, health care. Their plight fails to generate the same level of righteous indignation as abortion. Many churches recoil from issues of race. If churches want to respond to the current crisis, we must speak out against all forms of oppression against human life. This means decrying injustice, protesting alongside minorities, pressuring politicians to do justly, and challenging racism when it rears its ugly head in their local congregation.(6)

In the past 2016 presidential election, white evangelicals joined in with radical groups, led by racism and hatred, to prioritize their choice and strengthen the support of a white candidate who would endorse their combined interests of white supremacy. This group walked across moral, social, spiritual and denomination lines to unify as one voice for a candidate known to be racist and immoral. Once elected, this leader and his staff of similar mindset begun to immediately disband the programs that were established to help equalize rights and benefits of the ethnic community with those of the majority white population. The religious leaders, who both lead and receive ministry support from blacks, who were among those that elected the leader were silent at this dismantling. Ethnic groups suffer from removal of such programs and their votes casted for this candidate contribute to their own hurt. The John Perkins' article further illustrated that not only do blacks suffer, but so do poor whites.

> "Sometimes we would visit the local church, which distributed food to people in need. While the food was from the government and food networks, this simple operation was run by black folks at the church who had part of the civil rights movement and knew how to address needs in the community.
>
> Not just blacks came for food. Many poor whites came too. Sometimes when I visited the church, I would just hang back and watch the people come and go as they picked up food items. I always found the behavior of the white people quite curious. Their body language showed so much shame. One would almost think they were stealing the food.
>
> The poor whites didn't really have anything going for them except their whiteness and the fact that blacks had to say "Yes, Sir" and "No, Sir" to them. Since that was about all they had, they held on to it real tight. That's why I developed a strong dislike of poor white folks for a while—they were the ones who did most of the damage to blacks in rural Mississippi. For example, the deputies who beat me in jail were poor whites. They had a little bit of authority and a black man to hate. I was

one person who was lower than them in society, and they took out all their anger and fear and insecurity on me."(4)

Our political leaders, who are making decisions concerning the social, financial and health wellbeing of ethnic people and the poor, may not care about this damage to the already suffering people, but God cares and has the final word. Ministers are expected to be His hands and voice in the community to care about the needs of all God's children. But when ministers fail to uphold their responsibilities, it does not stop God from finding a way to help His children and all the poor and needy. God sets up leaders and pull down leaders as it suits His plan.

NO RACE IS PERFECT OR PURE

The Christian faith expects the believer to express faith in their religious leaders and the gospel they teach but it also requires them to pray, listen to the Spirit of God and study along with the leader's teaching to prevent the hazard of false teaching. Once one has come to Christ, the Holy Spirit provides guidance to lead one into deeper truths. Where difficult decisions are to be made, reliance on the Holy Spirit and the word should be the path to ultimate truth. We have seen examples of blind faith in leaders of various races who turned out to be cult leaders where people were led away from their culture and family support, e.g., Jim Jones or David Koresh. Though Christ does not state that a minister must be of the same culture or nationality as the congregation he leads, Christ gave us warnings in the word, provided multi-level church leadership and guidance by the Holy Spirit so that there would always be proper representation of righteousness, truth and liberty in the body of Christ to protect all people. The Holy Spirit in the church is the mind of Christ expressed in the body of believers and He knows every heart. Where the voice of Christ is silenced and a single leader is given total power, we will continue to see abuse and examples like that of the Jim Jones cult that led many blacks, whites, educated and uneducated people to their deaths in the backwoods of Jonestown, Guyana.

People can be equally guilty by refusing to listen to Christian ministers outside their own culture and, thereby, miss out on teachings available in the general body of Christ. Some churches become cults because they refuse any additional knowledge than what their minister teaches and that can also threaten the safety of the minister and the people. Such an example was a black man named Father Divine (1907-1965 ministry), who taught his people that he was God. The members of his church blindly followed him in error. All such examples can be avoided through obedience in personal reading and study of the word. The bible teaches the Christian congregation to follow godly examples, study scriptures for themselves, follow the teachings of Christ and obey the Holy Spirit. Where there is no evidence of God's presence, people should not feel obligated to follow the leader. The word of God never tells a people to put aside their own mind and blindly follow any leader. We are to observe their lives lived for God. Jesus challenged the Pharisees to search the scriptures to see that His ministry was true (Joh 5:39) and to believe Him because His works bore witness of Him. Paul defended his ministry with evidence of his work that aligned with Scripture. Jesus openly warned and gave examples of wolves and false leaders that would come and how they would behave toward the believer. People can be led astray due to ignorance as Jesus said. But knowing that people are subject to this error, they are safer in following the lifestyles of ministers whose lives they can observe and follow. Some people will still follow ministers after they have been exposed as unfaithful proving their error is not deception, but ignorance.

The main purpose of following ministers of one's own culture in one's own community is that the lives of their ministers should be visible, evaluated by the community they serve, and should witness whether or not they are true followers of Christ. The teachings of Christ should be leading that body of believers somewhere. The minister's life should witness an example of where he is leading his church members. Is Christ Lord over his life? Is his soul prospering spiritually in Christ? If the minister's life has become extravagant or dishonoring to Christ, it should be apparent to the congregation that the minister serves. So the minister should be visible among the flock. The minister should be living on a level where he is able to feel the infirmities of his people, like Christ witnessed while living among them. Here are some of the instructions given to ministers.

> Remember them that are in bonds, as bound with them; and them which suffer adversity, as being yourselves also in the body. Heb 13:3

> Feed the flock of God which is among you, taking the oversight *thereof,* not by constraint, but willingly; not for filthy lucre (money*), but of a ready mind; Neither as being lords over *God's* heritage, but being ensamples to the flock. 1Pe 5:2-3 (*Author's input of definition)

Paul spoke of how he bore the care of all the churches (II Cor 11:28). He made clear the destiny he was leading them to. The minister should not have the excuse that he is of a different culture and that different rules apply to him as a result. The same methods the minister used to arrive at Christian maturity should be available to the members of his congregation. Some people teach that the ground at the foot of the cross is level for all people, denoting no special privileges. The early Christian church equalized the wealth of the church by the willingness of those that had wealth sharing substance with those that had not. The prosperity gospel is in direct opposition with this practice. Those ministers boast of their materials wealth as an example of what the people can have by giving offerings to the minister. The church should be able to follow the same steps as the minister to receive blessings. Paul taught and illustrated this with his followers. The teachings of Christ in the bible and the Holy Spirit guides one into knowing the difference between truth and the ways of the wicked so that he is not led in sin or error.

There are so many nations and ethnicities and God is aware of all of them. Just like people have different languages and traditions, they also have different destinies. Some people are part of a people where there is a particular destiny of prophecy for them. Knowing history and heritage allows one to come into fulfillment of their prophesied destiny or break curses pronounced upon the group. Some races may have identifiable character traits whether good or evil. The children of Israel had a destiny and promise upon them that had to be worked out in time. Jacob prophesied both good and bad concerning his children (Gen 49) and they would walk out those pronouncements.

Every race of people is made in God's image; but they are also born into sin and shaped in iniquity, possessing the power to serve God or Satan. Some nations, like the Amorites, were particularly evil in God's sight. Jonathan, though dead, had a covenant that protected his last seed through his friendship with David. Esau threw away destiny in ignorance. The tribe of Dan was disinherited. So people as ethnicities, races or nations may have outstanding characteristics or destinies that God has a plan for. Daniel understood Jeremiah's prophecy about the years in the desolations of Jerusalem. The Israeli nation, though they sinned and were a disappointment to God, still have a grace upon them because of the covenant between God and Abraham.

One of the signs of the anti-Christ that is to appear in the last days will be his efforts to unify all people into a fleshy one-world religious experience where he will rule over them. Personal identities and ethnicities will not matter so that all people are accepted in the one church. What people will not do willingly for Christ, they will be forced to do for the anti-Christ. Christ is already Lord over His people regardless of their location, ethnicity, culture, traditions or physical characteristics. Christ rules in the spirit over His people and they obey His voice when He speaks. They do not have to all be in the same place, under one roof or guided by a single pastor to be His. Their unity is a spiritual unity submitted under the Father. Though there are believers from many different nations under one roof, their unity would be one of love for Jesus and the Father, not one of fleshy union or mental agreement. They are united in the spirit and accepted in the body of Christ regardless of location. Satan is an imitator of Christ and he perverts the truth to deceive the unlearned. The anti-Christ will try to bring all people into a one world false religious unity that disregards physical characteristics. He is trying now in the dark to reshape America and other nations for his one-world system and he does not care if false Christians help him through a false unity. The following Psalm of David expresses the sentiments of many Christian hearts.

Why Do You Hide Yourself?
Psalms 10

> Why standest thou afar off, O LORD? why hidest thou thyself in times of trouble? The wicked in his pride doth persecute the poor: let them be taken in the devices that they have imagined. For the wicked boasteth of his heart's desire, and blesseth the covetous, whom the LORD abhorreth. The wicked, through the pride of his countenance, will not seek after God: God is not in all his thoughts. His ways are always grievous; thy judgments are far above out of his sight: as for all his enemies, he puffeth at them. He hath said in his heart, I shall not be moved: for I shall never be in adversity. His mouth is full of cursing and deceit and fraud: under his tongue is mischief and vanity. He sitteth in the lurking places of the villages: in the secret places doth he murder the innocent: his eyes are privily set against the poor. He lieth in wait secretly as a lion in his den: he lieth in wait to catch the poor: he doth catch the poor, when he draweth him into his net. He croucheth, and humbleth himself, that the poor may fall by his strong ones. He hath said in his heart, God hath forgotten: he hideth his face; he will never see it. Arise, O LORD; O God, lift up thine hand: forget not the humble. Wherefore doth the wicked contemn God? he hath said in his heart, Thou wilt not require it. Thou hast seen it; for thou beholdest mischief and spite, to requite it with thy hand: the poor committeth himself unto thee; thou art the helper of the fatherless. Break thou the arm of the wicked and the evil man: seek out his wickedness till thou find none. The LORD is King for ever and ever: the heathen are perished out of his land. LORD, thou hast heard the desire of the humble: thou wilt prepare

> their heart, thou wilt cause thine ear to hear: To judge the fatherless and the oppressed, that the man of the earth may no more oppress.

SALVATION FOR EVERY NATION

The plan of God is to save every nation and ethnicity across the world. The royal priesthood of Israel was to be the preachers to the whole world; but in their failure, God sent Jesus to make salvation available for everyone that was lost regardless of their heritage. At Pentecost, the message was sent into all nations. The first apostles were given a command to preach the gospel to every nation and that command is still for the church.

> And they sung a new song, saying, Thou art worthy to take the book, and to open the seals thereof: for thou wast slain, and hast redeemed us to God by thy blood out of every kindred, and tongue, and people, and nation; Rev 5:9

> And when the day of Pentecost was fully come, they were all with one accord in one place. And suddenly there came a sound from heaven as of a rushing mighty wind, and it filled all the house where they were sitting. And there appeared unto them cloven tongues like as of fire, and it sat upon each of them. And they were all filled with the Holy Ghost, and began to speak with other tongues, as the Spirit gave them utterance. And there were dwelling at Jerusalem Jews, devout men, out of every nation under heaven. Now when this was noised abroad, the multitude came together, and were confounded, because that every man heard them speak in his own language. Act 2:1-6

> Go ye therefore, and teach <u>all nations</u>, baptizing them in the name of the Father, and of the Son, and of the Holy Ghost… Mat 28:19

> And this gospel of the kingdom shall be <u>preached in all the world</u> for a witness unto all nations; and then shall the end come…Mat 24:14

The true gospel message must reach every nation before Christ comes to take the church with Him to heaven. Therefore the gospel message must go out through true disciples who can reach people of all ethnicities, language and culture. One race of people do not have the capacity to reach or disciple the whole world because of an inability to communicate in every language or to convey understanding to all people from various backgrounds and beliefs. God did not intend for one race to rule over every other ethnicity but we are seeing the white race attempt world rule and dominance. God was the ruler of the Israelites and Christ is the ruler of the church. The gospel must be delivered by those that are able to communicate to their own peer group in a way that they can understand. In order for every nation and ethnicity to be reached, many types of ministers must become saved and then sent to their own people with the truth of the gospel. People must not just hear the message but they must be perfected by the gospel. The false belief system of the hearer must be overcome and every obstacle and false belief pulled down so that salvation can come to the whole man. This work is best done by those that can relate to the environment of the lost. It is not enough just to preach faith in Christ but a complete work must be done in the individual's heart and life.

DIVERSE NEEDS OF MINISTRY

When Israel was about to die, he prayed and prophesied over each of the children of Israel their future. The Prophet Isaiah prophesied the future and fate of various nations as did Ezekiel and other prophets. In Revelations, John went down the list of churches and prophesied about each of their judgment. We see in each of these end time prophesies that God is concerned about every nation and people. He had a plan and expectation of each and prophesied His destiny. This lets us know that God is concern about each ethnic group of people and they will be judged by His laws. He will judge us individually and as groups, e.g. ethnicity, city, state or nation. That is why it is so important that every nation is reached with the gospel to fulfill their destiny. The importance of salvation for every nation and people means that their ethnic questions and cultural practices that conflict with God's truth must be pulled down and the truth unfolded to them. Deliverance from error, cultic and demonic powers must be broken over those that have practiced witchcraft and other strange arts as well. The everyday American Christian cannot reach many of these people to wrestle their unbelief and practices. God has ordained in His plan for people to minister to them. Christ is the answer for every soul but does not speak to or use everyone alike. A prosperity gospel will not transform them and nor will a healing ministry. Their entrenchment in occultism must be met with truth that roots up the lies they have been fed by the devil so that they can be transformed into the image of Christ and join their fellow believers in the joy of the Lord.

Pseudo Christianity or a powder puff religion will not deliver people from the clutches of Satan's grip. Paul the apostle was so entrenched in his pharisaical beliefs that it took an encounter with Christ Himself to set him free. Few people have dared come up against such a furious opponent. Joseph was cunning before becoming a man of God and heir to the Abrahamic blessings. An angel was sent to wrestle with him. There are some people thought to be so bad that no one wants to wrestle with them but their soul is important to God. For every soul destined for heaven, regardless of how demented, someone must reach them for Christ. We cannot powder puff them or give a watered-down gospel that will not convict. Their self-will must be wrestled to the ground and the church cannot just pass them by for convenience sake.

Those nations that have been abused, exploited and persecuted by European nations and America must be reached and their emotional damage must be healed. Every ethnic people must have their issues resolved in the power of God that heals and makes us whole. That healing helps us to be able to relate to other ethnic groups or the dominant majority in a reconciled love so our culture no longer clashes but blend. Churches unwilling to get into the mud with them and fight for their souls and introduce Christ, should just look on or pray rather than try to soothe these people with a pseudo gospel that will not save. It takes the power of God to save and people must break up the fallow ground (Jer. 4:3).

The gospel "scripture is given by inspiration of God, and is profitable for doctrine, for reproof, for correction, for instruction in righteousness: That the man of God may be perfect, thoroughly furnished unto all good works (16-17). In every soul that comes to Christ, He has promised to do a perfect work in them. The Holy Spirit does the work but the church is assigned a role in perfecting the saints through the multi-level spiritual offices and gifting in the church. The church must receive the broken and bruised for Christ's sake and they must work with each saint to bring them to perfection. Not every church is equipped with power or willing to do the messy work of deliverance, yet that is the responsibility of the true church of God.

The cross was not pretty but it was necessary. Each child must have a cross experience and every child of God needs spirit-filled sisters, brothers, mothers and leaders to help them come through full deliverance and into the peace of Christ that is the mission the church and it is a mystery how it is performed. We can be certain though that it is done by the Holy Spirit's love. "How beautiful are the feet of them that preach the gospel of peace, and bring glad tidings of good things (Rom 10:15)!

HINDRANCES THAT PREVENT UNITY

We all know that there are so many different opinions and ways of life that conflict with other cultures but our dilemma is how we can overcome them. In the church age, the church is actually expected to be the tool used in the world to bring harmony among people and their vast opinions and ways. The gospel of Jesus Christ is given to bring man into harmony with God and other men. However, there is a problem that prevents our churches from coming together to solve human issues. Even though all Protestant churches and some other denominations preach Jesus, there is still little agreement with each other. Churches conflict over doctrine about baptism methods, tongues, dress, leadership style and worship. Jesus gave His disciples the Holy Spirit to infill, teach and empower them with God's ability to that they could be qualified and just ambassadors for Him to all mankind. The Holy Spirit as teacher, Comforter and Guide has the assignment to continue working in men to bring them to perfection. The Holy Spirit, as the other parts of Divinity, is perfect and without error or weakness. However, man is able to accept or resist the power of the Holy Spirit working in him to bring him to divine love. Therefore, the work of the Holy Spirit in church leaders is not without flaws. Our task then becomes to understand what it is that hinders God's work in the man of God that prevents advancing to the place of perfection. The minister must overcome his hindrances to lead the church into perfection.

The two foremost enemies of man, even the Spirit-filled man, are the flesh and the devil. But when man is operating in life, he is guided either by his spirit or mind. Man must choose and fight to promote the leadership of God over the devil's influence. The devil does his work through one of man's faculties to get man to do his will. We make the decision to succumb or resist the devil from using us. When the Holy Spirit is in charge of man's mind and body, God is able to lead man into His perfect will. Few men, however, yield total control to the Spirit of God working in him because it requires submission of man's pride and a life of humility. Most men, whether saved or not, are led by either their flesh or mind. If he is walking by his flesh, he has little hope of obeying God because the flesh is carnal and enmity against God. Not all churches believe that they are supposed to have the Holy Spirit working inside to guide them to the ways of God. Some churches teach that they are in filled with the Holy Spirit as soon as they acknowledge Jesus, yet Paul and the early church saw a continuous struggle with the flesh and progression into more power and infillings after accepting Christ. So we can see that the teachings and practices of the church lead us into beliefs that vastly differ from other churches.

Pastors that appear successful in ministry are actually being led by the Spirit of God or through an educated mind that is obedient to its teaching. Man has to take rein over his flesh and the devil to walk in stability in his life. Spirit-led men must have this stability and more to be led of God. Spirit-led pastors must have their whole man under submission to the Spirit of God. It is not easy to manage control over the strong will of the flesh or a worldly mind but it is possible. The apostles taught how we must overcome our worldly life. Our mental processes can learn obedience and submission to the Spirit; and it does require their submission for God to lead. A learned man can come to the place of a spiritual man (like Saul), though his intellect will still resist any guidance that does not also provide understanding. God requires us to come to Him as a little child but educated men require knowledge and understanding before complying. Therein is the problem with many educated men who cannot follow God's ways. Paul was a much learned man but he put all his knowledge on the altar and counted it as dung so that he could win Christ (Php. 3:7-8). Our educational system and many religious schools have been corrupted with ungodly principles. Educational facilities not only give the student many opinions to consider in their study but successful passage through their programs require acceptance of their information and thought process. Some of them return from bible training or colleges as atheists. Many programs are established by some man's interpretation of what God has said. All that go through their programs must accept their thoughts for mastery, whether right or wrong. Those that are religious leaders teach whole churches, denominations or other preachers what they now believe and the truth may have never been disclosed.

Despise the seemingly impossibility of the truth penetrating this mountain of error, God can give man truth that pulls down a mountain of falsehoods and work in man's mind to deliver him from error, like He did in Pharisaical Saul. There is a certain amount of humility and suffering required to be a true child of God that men tend to shy away from. Christ suffered much pain and humiliation to become our Savior and men of God must imitate Christ is this as well, just like Paul and other apostles.

CHRISTIANITY MUST BRING TRUTH

America that started out with a Christian influence has reached a place where it wants to throw off that influence and fly loose with only its own opinion to follow. We are seeing our nation act like a teenage girl who wants to throw off parental guidance and do her own thing. We could all write the devastating end of that story so why would we allow our nation to take the same course? We must continue the course of Christianity but we must also perfect that walk. Christian leaders must start practicing the gospel they preach and perfect a righteous walk that they can teach their church members. America was established by leaders who planned beyond their own lives and interests to preserve the nation. Prejudice and bigotry need to be purged out of a fleshly walk so that one can walk in the spirit. Christianity in America must move forward so that the nation can progress.

A life must by purified by the Holy Spirit and every stronghold must be pulled down so that liberty in Christ is experienced in true holiness. The mind will have to be challenged as was necessary for Paul, a learned Pharisee full of the Law's objections to grace. When Paul was going through the land, as the most zealous Pharisees to stop the spread of Christianity, he was unstoppable in his rage. Peter was the strongest spiritual Christian at that time but the scriptures also revealed his cowardice in denying Christ and standing up as a defense for the gentile believers when Jews came into the gathering. He was probably not the best candidate to reach the heart of a zealous Pharisee trying to wipe out Christians. No, Jesus took on that mission Himself and brought Saul to his knees in one visitation. On the Damascus Road, Saul's encounter with the risen Christ caused him to ask who are thou Lord. Jesus answered, "I am Jesus whom thou persecuteth?" Saul said, "Lord, what wilt thou have me to do?" Man meeting the true power of God, can do nothing but submit. Jesus answered, "Arise and go into the city and it shall be told thee what thou must do." This was the end of the rage of Saul and the beginning of the Christian mission of Apostle Paul. Jesus brought down the strongest enemy of the Christians. Jesus is still bringing down the strongest enemies of Christianity by appearing to radical

Muslims and others who are seeing visions of Christ and being converted to salvation. This type of deliverance is also in response to the prayers of the saints. Remember Peter was miraculously set free from the prison by the prayers of the saints. God is working among many groups to bring salvation but the primary way He has given us to reach the lost of any group we encounter is through witnessing. After Saul's strength was broken through the encounter with Jesus on the Damascus Road, Paul was directed by Jesus to go to a place where a Christian disciple would heal his eyes and bring him into the fellowship of the Christians. "And straightway he preached Christ in the synagogues, That he is the Son of God (Acts 9:20)." The Christians were then free to continue their witnessing without Saul's terror.

Jesus is still trying to reach the staunchest of radicals against Christianity that disrupts our peaceful existence. Sometimes He personally intervenes but most often He sends us. The story of David Wilkerson as a young minister from Pennsylvania (1958) who was sent to New York to witness to a radical gang in New York shows Christ is still reaching zealots and bringing them to salvation. In this story, Nicky Cruz was the gang leader with an ethnic group. He was Hispanic and the minister sent to him was white. The story of Nicky Cruz's encounter with Christ is described in the book: "The Cross, The Switchblade, and the Man Who Believed" by David Wilkerson. God wants to reach ethnic groups and he uses those that know Him to reach out to ethnic people that do not, like in the model of Peter, Paul and many early disciples. The best method is to reach ethnic people is through the Christian conversion of one of them who can reach his own peer group. Another story of an outreach to an ethnic group is told in Chapter 10 of Acts. A gentile man named Cornelius, a centurion of the band called the Italian band.

> A devout man, and one that feared God with all his house, which gave much alms to the people, and prayed to God alway. He saw in a vision evidently about the ninth hour of the day an angel of God coming in to him, and saying unto him, Cornelius. And when he looked on him, he was afraid, and said, What is it, Lord? And he said unto

> him, Thy prayers and thine alms are come up for a memorial before God. And now send men to Joppa, and call for one Simon, whose surname is Peter: He lodgeth with one Simon a tanner, whose house is by the sea side: he shall tell thee what thou oughtest to do. Act 10:2-6

This man's prayers reached God and he was to send for Peter who would preach the gospel to him. Now Peter knew the Jews were not to go to gentile groups according to the Law and the instructions of Jesus to His disciples. But Peter had a visitation from the Lord to change this policy and not to call any man God has cleansed common or unclean. Peter went to Cornelius as Jesus instructed but told Cornelius of this rule of Jews in Acts 10:28, 29.

The response of Cornelius to the arrival of Peter was to "call together his kinsmen and near friends (Acts 10:24)." Peter then proceeded (Act 10:34-35) "I perceive that God is no respecter of persons. But in every nation he that feareth him, and worketh righteousness, is accepted with him." Cornelius family and friends were baptized after hearing the gospel and were filled with the Holy Spirit. They asked Peter to stay and he remained with them for a time. When the church heard the gentiles received the gospel, their response was to send forth mature Christians or apostles to preach Jesus to the new believers. They sent Barnabus, who departed to seek Paul, and they taught the new church the word for a whole year. The people of Antioch were first to be called Christians. Paul and Barnabus went from place to place preaching the word. They taught the gentiles but it was their own Jewish nation that rose up against inclusion of gentiles into the faith (Acts 13:45). Paul's practice was to regularly preach Jesus and strongly persuade the staunchest Jew about the truth of Jesus and inclusion of gentiles into the faith. This seems to be the role that white Christian America is missing. This scripture clearly shows the responsibility of the Christian leadership to deal with the radical division being brought about from their own sect. White Christian America is not taking this lead on racial issues and abating the hatred with a witness of the love Jesus gives. The power of God is manifested in the church of Jesus Christ for the purpose of standing against the satanical hatred being shown in the land. That power should not be kept within the walls of the church for member's rejoicing only. It is the power of God to break down walls and heal hurt. Ministers must instruct and guide the people into using the power of God as Jesus instructed us to make a difference in our world. We are the body of Christ and Christ's power goes everywhere we go witnessing the love of Jesus.

When the Jews tried to indoctrinate the gentiles into Jewish traditions Paul and Barnabus debated them until the decision was made to take the matter to the apostles for a group decision. The apostles and elders met and their decision was that Jewish traditions would not be imposed on gentile believers except to encourage them to restrain from fornication, things strangled and blood. So the Jewish apostles determined that their traditions and rites would not be imposed on other cultures (Acts 15:19-20, 26-29). Here is an example for American Christians. These Spirit-filled leaders got together and actually sought a solution and found a resolution for the dispute. Is Christ less powerful today?

Contrary to thc practicc of the early Christians, what we are seeing in American Christianity is that Americans are transporting and imposing their Christian worship, teachings and traditions to every nation. White Christian evangelists dominate the market with their books, music and videos. The whole world is being led into their doctrine and ways through multi-media international outlets. The question that remains though is whether we are seeing true disciples being made from the multitudes of dollars and effort. Despite all these Christian broadcasts, the nation and world is still in turmoil. The debauchery of this generation of Christians has declined into the practices of pre-Christian times. Racial hatred is at an all-time high and unbelievers want no part of a superficial religion. Unlike the early Jewish apostles, our generation of popular Christian leaders have not squashed or subdued their own ranks of zealots against inclusion of other races and nations into the body of Christ or Christian society. This void shows where the white Christians should direct their efforts and dollars: onto outreach among their own people and perfecting their faith. Instead they have more recently joined ranks with white supremacy zealots to elect a national leader who himself supports and legislates policies that are anti-Christian in respect to the love and provision Christ promises to all believers and who advocate for white nationalism. This is the manifested fruit of their long efforts in Christianity.

Apostle Paul and the other apostles and disciples in Jerusalem were able to solve problems because they had legitimate conversion from Christ that gave them genuine power to affect the problems of their day. Paul wrote out for us in the book of Romans how the saints must fight to overcome the power of the world, flesh and the devil. The flesh has to be overcome and trained to restrain from fleshy ways. Salvation is necessary for spirit, soul and body and it takes ministry to bring about a matured soul ready for Christ's kingdom. The challenges that the mind and flesh present against salvation are best met by someone who is able to teach the newly born again soul the ways of God from scripture and experience. It is a struggle to put off the old nature and become fully submitted to Christ. There is a factor of suffering that must be embraced to become a true Christian (II Tim. 2:12). One who has met with such challenges is best able to teach a newly saved person how to stand for Christ.

The reason Christ came to earth was to be a witness to us that we can obey and overcome evil because Christ was subjected to the same temptations in the flesh, yet without sin. He overcame them through the Spirit, prayer and obedience to the Father. He put on a body of flesh to be an example of obedience for us to witness. In like manner, those of our own ethnicity must show us how they overcame the same temptations we experience. A visible witness with us was so important that God put on a flesh body, came to dwell among us and subjected Himself to the same temptations of sin and the devil as we experience to show us the way to overcome. Identification with the hearer is just that important and we cannot overlook this advantage. Anyone can witness to us salvation but making a disciple for Christ requires much more time and effort on the part of the minister. It is not easy because the believer's soul and flesh fights to hold on to the old life. They must be challenged and reasoned with by our witness until they submit to the truth and accept the Lordship of Christ over their desire.

There are so many people that are professing Christ who have never submitted to His Lordship because they have not overcome the flesh's desire or a worldly mind. Paul recorded that he wished us to be prosperous spirit, soul and body. Some people may make it to heaven but lose out in this world the battle of the mind or body against sin. Jesus walked with his Jewish disciples as a Jew and dealt with everything His followers had to deal with. When asked about liberty from taxes while under a Roman occupation, he had an answer because he was subjected to the same rule as they. He submitted to the law as we are advised to do. As the disciples watched Him deal with every aspect of the Jewish life and salvation, they were able to follow the pattern in similar fashion. Jesus and Paul taught the importance of following their example into salvation and how to walk with God. We learn to live for God through watching the ministers and saints before us overcome challenges until we are able to follow the footsteps of Christ for ourselves. John led his disciples all the way to Christ where he released them to continue the journey by following Christ alone. Ministers must give an example, pattern or footsteps that their followers can imitate behind them. Members must not be told at any point that the follower must do something different because the minister is special or in a different class from them. This would give reason and excuse for disbelief to the follower and be a hindrance to salvation. Jesus constantly called His disciples His "brethren". They lived in the same land, had the same requirements as He and could follow His guidelines all the way to the Father. The disciples did follow the pattern of Christ even to the death and are promised seats on 12 thrones in eternity (Mat 19:28). Christ provided a pattern that could be followed and He successfully keeps His disciples until the end.

While Christ does not prefer one race above another in the New Testament days, He does give us an example of ministry that is worthy of our following. Racial prejudice is not condoned by Christ and He has shown us that love is the best way to live. Once we witness to our own house and community of our own ethnicity and put on Christ, we become part of the church at large and are brethren in Christ with the same rights and privileges as the rest of the body. We then have a greater mission and calling to reach a large audience for Christ. It is though the love of Christ that we are all brought into "one fold" as the church without regard to ethnicity or culture. There is sameness in Christ that defies the lines of ethnicity, culture or nation. Love brings us into the spirit of oneness that God has ordained through Christ. We are all made like God in the spirit and the spirit has no regard for the physical appearance of any man.

In heaven, believers will know each other to a greater degree than here on earth and earthly physical characteristics and designation will have no meaning in the equality of heaven. This state is bought out in Galatians 3:28. That is the way it is supposed to be in the church now but love must do its perfect work to bring it to pass. Jesus sent out ministers with particular assignments to special places and people but they would all eventually be brought in to one fold like on Noah's ark where the animals filed in two or three at a time until all were on board. The animals shared no similarities except they were all called to one place. God's desire is to save the whole world and He has set His ministers in every nation and culture to bring in the souls of every ethnicity and nation. None are to be ostracized, demeaned or denied their rightful privileges in Christ and the Kingdom. We witness in scripture how the apostles were sent from nation to nation to declare Jesus Christ as the Risen Lord. The disciples of every ethnicity went out to preach the gospel to every land in the world. During the time of the early church, the word had gone out to the entire known world and churches were springing up and flourishing as the people grew into the body of Christ. We must do this work afresh in every generation until Jesus comes.

The scriptures listed below reveal the purpose of the gospel message and God's desires for all people:

> God that made the world and all things therein, seeing that he is Lord of heaven and earth, dwelleth not in temples made with hands; Neither is worshipped with men's hands, as though he needed any thing, seeing he giveth to all life, and breath, and all things; And hath made of one blood all nations of men for to dwell on all the face of the earth, and hath determined the times before appointed, and the bounds of their habitation… Act 17:24-26

> And he gave some, apostles; and some, prophets; and some, evangelists; and some, pastors and

> teachers; For the perfecting of the saints, for the work of the ministry, for the edifying of the body of Christ: Till we all come in the unity of the faith, and of the knowledge of the Son of God, unto a perfect man, unto the measure of the stature of the fulness of Christ: That we *henceforth* be no more children, tossed to and fro, and carried about with every wind of doctrine, by the sleight of men, *and* cunning craftiness, whereby they lie in wait to deceive; But speaking the truth in love, may grow up into him in all things, which is the head, *even* Christ: From whom the whole body fitly joined together and compacted by that which every joint supplieth, according to the effectual working in the measure of every part, maketh increase of the body unto the edifying of itself in love. Eph 4:11-16

> Neither pray I for these alone, but for them also which shall believe on me through their word; That they all may be one; as thou, Father, *art* in me, and I in thee, that they also may be one in us: that the world may believe that thou hast sent me. And the glory which thou gavest me I have given them; that they may be one, even as we are one: I in them, and thou in me, that they may be made perfect in one; and that the world may know that thou hast sent me, and hast loved them, as thou hast loved me. Joh 17:20-23

Since the breakup of the fellowship between God and the first humans in the Garden of Eden, it has been the plan of God to bring all people that have been divided and disbursed across the nations back into a restored fellowship of obedience with Him. Jesus expressed clearly in John 17:21. "That they all may be one; as thou, Father, art in me, and I in thee, that they also may be one in us…, that they may be made perfect in one…"

Diversity in the family occurred after the fall and the sin nature has perpetuated a jealousy and hatred among people because of these diversities. The church must overcome racial prejudice, pride, and spirits of racial superiority, greed oppression, hatred, partiality and a false gospel to enter into the kingdom of God and witness Christ to the world. The kingdom of God does not have second-class citizens and none are authorized to Lord over another. The church must hear the heart of God: "Is not this the fast that I have chosen? to loose the bands of wickedness, to undo the heavy burdens, and to let the oppressed go free, and that ye break every yoke? Is it not to deal thy bread to the hungry, and that thou bring the poor that are cast out to thy house? when thou seest the naked, that thou cover him; and that thou hide not thyself from thine own flesh?" (Isa 58:6-7) Where the witness between groups is tainted by self-will, dominion intents, race rule, or wealth; it is not Christ-like and will not produce true Christians or unity. The church must hear where it has erred and correct error, returning to God who will heal the land. Christ said He was our brethren and no man can claim more authority or a higher seat than He. The plan of God was to bring all people groups and diversities back into a love relationship with God through the finished work of Christ so that these differences would no longer matter to a perfected people. We assume different offices in the church to fulfill certain roles that bring Christian unity in the body, but Christ declared that we are all brethren. The church's failure to overcome the work of the flesh and flow in the love of Christ has hindered the church and the nations from the healing we should have accomplished. The work of the church was to cultivate in each person, family, neighborhood, city, state, and nation of the world a love experience, a version of the Garden of Eden where God could fellowship with every person like He did the first family. God established a way in which it was to be done and it can still be accomplished by an obedient church that follows the Spirit of God.

The love shown in the upper room church that saturated their neighbors and city is still available to overflow in our communities as well. Believers need to pray about the failure they see in their church and then purpose to help make things different. It is possible for one person to make things better. The faithfulness of a believer, named Daniel, who lived as a prisoner in a hostile and idolatrous nation, was able through his faith and testimony to point that nation to God. Members of Christian churches put too much emphasis on the position of pastor and not enough on their ability through God to make a major difference in our society. Each person should use the Spirit of God inside to affect his own world through witness and testimony. God has a special work for every child of God to do and we each need to seek Him to find out what our role is in this needy world. Many people feel too weak or inept to step out and do a work for God, but it is Christ that does the work through us when we submit to His will. When the people of the church use their spiritual gifting for the Lord, the work of the church can be accomplished by each one using his gifting and doing his part to affect a portion of the world. Pastors need the prayers and the gifting of the members to fulfill the call of the church in the community as stated in Ephesian Chapter 4. We are all a part of the body and the work must be performed by our united effort. God is waiting on us to get in line with the Spirit so that He can pour out the Holy Spirit's power to restore the land, cleanse and unite the people of the earth in a heavenly love only seen in heaven on high. God is still waiting for the church to get up and do the work of God. They were not ordained to be pew warmers or a Sunday audience looking for a good show with lights and fireworks. Every member of the church has contact with a multitude of people daily and each can impact the world for Christ.

Confession: I have personally done street witness everywhere I lived. I enjoyed it and did not do it under compulsion. I understood we were to witness and originally the Spirit of God encouraged and gave me ideas for witnessing tracts. As a woman in a church that did not give an outlet to minister, it was my way of sharing the gospel. With my being so active in street witnessing, it stands to reason that God would eventually let me know if it was His perfect will. I had pondered over how to follow up with some of these most tender souls and where to direct them for further ministry. I usually recommended a selection of churches. I realized the need to help people toward spiritual birth and Christian fellowship so street witnessing did not do a complete job. The flaws in this system became more and more apparent. Like the good Father He is, God showed me His perfect will is what I will call situational witnessing. You are going to get some water and you ask someone for a dipper (or cup) and then you ask if you can tell them about the best water ever. Get the point? So witnessing is not testifying in church to the saints or street witnessing. It is sharing the gospel with family, friends and acquaintances along the way. Every child of God should be taught this kind of witnessing. I still do some street witness with a goal toward discipleship.

God scattered the people and confounded their language to prevent the united evil they people were determined to do. God desires for His people to unite and live in unity but in a unity of righteousness and love. When people make a concerted effort to live out love, it changes our world for the better. Churches are made up of people and it does make a difference what we do as an individuals. Pastors are important but ultimately it is the people in the congregation who determine the nature of the church. If people would assimilate the gospel and live out the gospel message with prayer and bible reading, churches would look more like Christ. We, as individual believers, have a remarkable ability to win souls through our daily witness in our community. If we would take the time to impact every person we encounter with a positive witness, we could do a great work for God. If we have a true conversion and are born again, Christ lives in us individually. We carry the love of God in us to touch people for Christ. We saw in Acts 8:27 the deacon, Philip, was dispatched to the roadside by an angel to preach Jesus to a eunuch of Ethiopia who sought to understand scripture. Philip preached Jesus and baptized the man after he confessed faith in Christ and requested it. Immediately after this, Philip was taken by the spirit away to another place where he continued preaching Jesus through the cities. God started this street witness and could be counted on to complete it. Here was a man newly appointed as a deacon in Chapter 6 who is a willing vessel being used by the Lord to affect Ethiopia and other cities. He is an example of how God wants to lead each of us from glory to glory for the benefit of the Kingdom of God.

COMMANDED TO WITNESS

> But ye shall receive power, after that the Holy Ghost is come upon you: and ye shall be witnesses unto me both in Jerusalem, and in all Judaea, and in Samaria, and unto the uttermost part of the earth. Act 1:8

> And he said unto them, Go ye into all the world, and preach the gospel to every creature. He that believeth and is baptized shall be saved; but he that believeth not shall be damned. And these signs shall follow them that believe; In my name shall they cast out devils; they shall speak with new tongues; They shall take up serpents; and if they drink any deadly thing, it shall not hurt them; they shall lay hands on the sick, and they shall recover. Mar 16:15-18

The scriptures above are the commands of Jesus to His disciples (that includes each of us) to serve as witness to others after receiving the Holy Spirit. The Holy Spirit was necessary to witness Christ because no man can say that Jesus is Lord but by the Holy Spirit (I Cor. 12:3). Once they had learned the truth they were compelled to teach others. The Holy Spirit allowed them to witness Christ with power in preaching, healing and setting free those in bondage. Jesus told His accusers if they did not believe He was the Messiah then believe Him for the miracles he worked. Our witness through the works of Christ is a confirmation of Christ living in us. The saints are also to lay hands on people for healing. Too many churches are failing to inform and prepare the church members as witnesses for Christ and we are seeing the evidence of this failure in our society. Church members, not just preachers, are expected by Christ to be daily witnesses. The Jehovah Witnesses are showing up the church, who is the true witness of Christ's divinity. Christians are empowered to be a witness everywhere they go. We do not have to do street witnessing. It would be enough if church members would just witness at home, on the job, in the neighborhood, at social events and in everyday conversations. The impact would be tremendous. It would improve the life of the Christian and the unbeliever. The blessings would be seen on both; and the community and world be reap the benefits as well.

Jesus Christ came as a living witness of God's love for us. He walked out a perfect witness of how we are to live for the Father. So in His life, we see the perfect example of witnessing. The majority of His witness was one on one with people as we saw in His witness to Andrew, Peter, Nicodemus, Zacchaeus, and the woman at the well. Jesus witnessed mostly to Jews and refused to minister at first to the woman of Canaan (Mt 15:22) but was persuaded by her faith, which qualified her for mercy. There were a variety of ways Jesus used to witness including stories, parables, healings, deliverance and resurrection from the dead and through preaching. He witnessed on the road, in homes, at dinner, by the sea, near the mountains, in the synagogue, and on the ship. Jesus chose some of His nation to teach and recruit as teachers for the Jews. He freely healed and delivered those that came to Him. He preached to crowds and then moved on to other places. He debated religious leaders and ministered to the poor and needy food and money. He had a positive impact on His environment and the people. Jesus fully expounded the gospel and spent much time answering questions. The disciples of Jesus followed His pattern of witnessing and established churches in many cities led by elders. Jesus and His disciples saw true conversion and fruit from their labor. Our witnessing should follow the examples given us in the scriptures. Every Christian can witness and should witness for Christ. That is how we can turn the world around for Christ one person at a time. Jesus witnessed everywhere because the people followed Him everywhere He went. The message is that our life becomes a witness and we actively give people the truth they need to escape hell and make heaven their home.

Bible history tells us of men whose lives were a witness and how they transformed cities or nations, e.g., Moses, Elijah, and Daniel. These heroes of the scripture had to overcome their own internal battles to become witnesses, leaders of men and change the course of their world. Witnessing has the power to change the world. How is your witness?

So teach us to number our days, that we may apply our hearts unto wisdom. Return, O LORD, how long? and let it repent thee concerning thy servants. O satisfy us early with thy mercy; that we may rejoice and be glad all our days. Make us glad according to the days wherein thou hast afflicted us, and the years wherein we have seen evil. Let thy work appear unto thy servants, and thy glory unto their children. And let the beauty of the LORD our God be upon us: and establish thou the work of our hands upon us; yea, the work of our hands establish thou it. Psa 90:12-17

References

(1) National Geographic News, Modern Humans Came Out of Africa, "Definitive" Study, July 18, 2007, James Owen.

(2) NY Times.com, "A Single Migration From Africa Populated the World, Studies Find", Carl Zimmer, September 21, 2016.

(3) Christianity Today, "Repenting of Superiority". Morgan Lee, June 2017.

(4) Christianity Today, "Evangelicals and Race – A New Chapter". Mark Galli. August 22, 2016.

(5) Christianity Today, "John Perkins: I Wish I Had Done More to Help Poor White People", John Perkins, March 21, 2017.

(6) Christianity Today, 'The Church at Its Racial Turning Point", Theon E. Hill, July 12, 2016

All scriptures taken from the King James Version of the Bible.

Other Books by the Author:

Elephant in the Room: The Economy and Whose Job It Is to Fix It

Silencing the Voice of the Prophet

The Father

Black Church Identity Crisis: Pimping the church

www.ingramcontent.com/pod-product-compliance
Ingram Content Group UK Ltd.
Pitfield, Milton Keynes, MK11 3LW, UK
UKHW040558210726
13854UKWH00008B/1496

9 781387 188253